GCSE

Susan Elkin

To Kill a
Mockingbird

Series Editor:
Steve Eddy

Philip Allan Updates
Market Place
Deddington
Oxfordshire
OX15 0SE
tel: 01869 338652
fax: 01869 337590
e-mail: sales@philipallan.co.uk
www.philipallan.co.uk

© Philip Allan Updates 2005

ISBN-13: 978-1-84489-227-3
ISBN-10: 1-84489-227-1

In all cases we have attempted to trace and credit copyright owners of material used.

Printed by Raithby, Lawrence & Co Ltd, Leicester

Environmental information
The paper on which this title is printed is sourced from mills using wood from managed, sustainable forests.

P00497

Contents

Study and revision

Context

Plot and structure

Characterisation

Themes

Style

Tackling the exam

Answers

Study and revision

Approaching the text

A novel is, above all, a narrative. A large part of the storyteller's art is to make you want to find out what happens next, and to keep you reading to the end. In order to study *To Kill a Mockingbird* and to enjoy it, you need to keep a close track of the events that take place. This guide will help you to do that, but you may also benefit from keeping your own notes about the main events and who is involved in them.

However, any novel consists of much more than its events. Although you need to know the story well to get a good grade in the exam, if you spend a lot of time simply retelling the story you will not get a high mark. You must be aware of a number of other features:

* You need to consider the setting of the novel — where the events take place — and how this influences the story.
* You need to get to know the characters and how the author, Harper Lee, tells us what they are like. Consider what they say and do, and what other people say about them. Also think about why they behave in the way they do — their motives — and what clues the author gives us about this.
* As you read on, you will also notice themes — the ideas explored by the author. You may find it easier to think about these while not actually reading the book, especially if you discuss them with other people.
* You should also try to become aware of the style of the novel, especially on a second reading — this means how the author tells the story.

The elements above are all dealt with in this guide. However, you should always try to notice them for yourself. This guide is no substitute for a careful and thoughtful reading of the text.

Revising the text

You will by now have read *To Kill a Mockingbird* at least once, almost certainly as part of classwork or homework, backed up by various lessons and tasks at school to help you understand and get to know the text. Your job now is to revise it for your GCSE examination.

The first thing to do is to reread the story to remind yourself what happens, who the characters are and how the novel is written. Ideally, before you take an English literature exam, you need to have read the text right through at least three times.

If you find it difficult to make yourself sit down to read, one possibility is to read one chapter a day alongside revision for other subjects. There are 31 chapters in *To Kill a Mockingbird*. At a rate of one chapter a day, that is one month's fairly light work. If you begin early, you could do that before you begin any more detailed revision.

Once you have reread the novel you can begin to revise in more depth. This means looking at the story more closely, chapter by chapter. Many students find that they know the beginning of a novel better than the end, perhaps because they have begun to reread it several times but have failed to finish it. One way around this when revising chapters is to start from the end and work backwards. You already know the story, so you should be able to pick it up anywhere and know what is going on. This technique will not work for everyone, but many GCSE students find it helpful. Another possibility is to start in the middle, say at Chapter 12 (the start of Part Two), and reread Part Two before going back to Part One.

Making the most of this guide

Read the Context section, which gives information on the historical, cultural and literary background of *To Kill a Mockingbird*. Most of what you write in your exam essay will relate directly to your reading of the text, but you will also get credit for showing that you understand something about the circumstances that gave rise to this novel. It is useful to know, for example, that Harper Lee came from Alabama herself and that the early 1930s was a period of hardship, particularly for blacks, who certainly did not have equality. Your insights into *To Kill a Mockingbird* will be much more perceptive if you make an effort to understand the place and period.

When you are revising the novel chapter by chapter, use the Plot and Structure section of this guide. Every novel has a shape, and *To Kill a Mockingbird* is particularly well crafted. The plot summaries will help you to make sure that you have grasped the key elements of each chapter.

Once you have reminded yourself of the plot, you need to think about the novel as a whole and to build on the work that you have done in class about characters, themes and style. It is helpful to think of the 'big picture'. Looking at individual chapters is the 'small picture', whereas looking at, say, how Harper Lee develops the theme of prejudice, or the character of Calpurnia, or suspense in her storytelling, are examples of the 'big picture'.

Look carefully at the information provided in the Characterisation, Themes and Style sections of this guide, but remember this is only a starting point. This guide does not contain everything you might need to write in an exam answer on *To Kill a Mockingbird*. Instead, it shows you what to look for — with plenty of examples. You should then, for example, be able to find other themes in the novel or other interesting aspects of Harper Lee's language.

This guide ends with advice about tackling the GCSE exam. It is best to work through the main body of the guide first before you look at this. Once you really know the novel well, answering the exam questions should not present too much difficulty for most students.

However, there are ways in which you can improve your essay-writing technique. Therefore, in the Tackling the Exam section you will find advice on how to begin and end essays and how to make the best use of quotations. This is followed by examples of grade C essays, which are then rewritten at the level of an A* answer to show you the difference.

At the end of each section 'Review your learning' questions are provided. Answers to the questions appear on pages 94–97.

> **Key point**
>
> Education, and particularly the study of English literature, is an unending journey. The more you look, and the more work you do, the more you find — and the more satisfying it is. That is why this guide asks questions and expects you to work out your own answers.

Watching the film

To Kill a Mockingbird was made into a famous black-and-white film (directed by Robert Mulligan) by Universal Studios in 1962, two years after the book was published. Harper Lee's novel had already won the Pulitzer Prize — an award given annually for fiction by an American author — and the actor Gregory Peck won a Best Actor Oscar for his performance as Atticus Finch in the film.

It is a fine film and in many ways true to the text. Mary Badham's portrayal of Scout is very faithful to the textual character. Harper Lee is said to have been so overcome by Peck's likeness to her father that she afterwards gave him her father's watch as a thank you gift and keepsake. Set designers travelled to Monroeville (see page 6) and made an almost exact replica of the county courthouse for the trial scene. So it is clear that a great deal of attention was paid to detail.

However, when you are studying a novel for an exam, films (and plays) based on the book have to be treated with caution. A film can only ever be *based* on a

novel. There are bound to be changes because what works on the printed page cannot always work in a visual medium.

For example, how could Scout's first-person narrative be conveyed on screen? Although the film uses a certain amount of 'voice over' to communicate this, for much of the time you simply see the children doing things and lose sight of the fact that the story is told by Scout. This is particularly apparent when, in the film, Scout goes with Jem, Calpurnia and Atticus to tell Helen Robinson that her husband Tom has been killed. In the novel, Scout stays at home and Dill tells her about it afterwards. Examiners are unimpressed by students who refer to the film rather than the text, and it is easy to make a mistake with this sort of detail if you have seen the film several times but read the novel only casually. Similarly, in the novel Atticus tells Scout that he has been asked by Judge Taylor to defend Tom. We do not 'see' the actual conversation. However, in the film the judge calls on Atticus and chats to him about it on his veranda.

Then there is the question of length. *To Kill a Mockingbird* is more than 300 pages long. The film runs for just over two hours. Inevitably, the director Robert Mulligan and the screenplay writer had to cut the plot drastically. This means that many details, characters and incidents, which you need to know about, are missing from the film. They include:

* the burning of Miss Maudie's house
* Aunt Alexandra
* the visit to First Purchase Church
* Mrs Dubose
* Link Deas
* Dolphus Raymond

Pause for thought

By 1962, films were usually made in colour. Why do you think Universal Studios chose to make *To Kill a Mockingbird* in black and white?

If you see the film and get too familiar with it before you have studied the text in depth, the film's strong visual messages can easily block out your memory of what is in the novel. It is therefore better to watch the film only after you have got to know the novel well. Then you can view it critically (and enjoyably) and work out for yourself why Mulligan made some of the decisions he did. Used in that way, the film will probably help with your understanding of the story.

There is also a play version of *To Kill a Mockingbird* adapted for the stage by Christopher Sergel.

Useful websites

The following websites could help you in your studies of *To Kill a Mockingbird*:

* www.universalteacher.org.uk/gcse/mockingbird.htm contains detailed notes on the novel and how to study it

* www.bbc.co.uk/schools/gcsebitesize/english_literature/prosemockingbird/index.shtml gives comprehensive notes on studying the novel
* www.lausd.k12.ca.us/Belmont_HS/tkm includes a detailed, chapter-by-chapter glossary of words likely to be unfamiliar, for example 'auspicious', 'scuppenongs' and 'melancholy' in Chapter 4
* www.quotegarden.com/bk-km.html is a useful list of quotes from the novel with chapter references
* http://mockingbird.chebucto.org/bio.html provides useful biographical information on Harper Lee

Context

> What is Harper Lee's background?
> Are her characters based on real people?
> What is the history of black people in the American South?
> Why were people particularly poor in the 1930s?
> What inspired Harper Lee to write the novel in the late 1950s?
> How does *To Kill a Mockingbird* relate to other fiction from the Southern states?

Fact and fiction

Harper Lee was born in Monroeville, Alabama, in 1926. She was the youngest of three children and her father was a lawyer.

Jean Louise ('Scout') Finch, the narrator of *To Kill a Mockingbird*, was born in the same year as her creator in a fictional Alabama town called Maycomb. Scout's father, Atticus, is a lawyer and she is the younger child in the family.

To Kill a Mockingbird is a good example of fiction that has developed from the author's personal experiences. Maycomb is based on Monroeville and Atticus is based on Harper Lee's own father.

Time Life Pictures/Getty Images

Harper Lee in the Monroeville courthouse, 1961

The character of Scout is probably much like the young Harper Lee. The author has freely admitted that she based the character of Dill on Truman Capote, another American novelist who grew up in Monroeville and was a childhood friend of hers.

Many of the places mentioned in the novel, such as Mobile, and the state capital Montgomery, are real. *The Mobile Register*, which Scout was 'born reading', and Atticus's favourite *Montgomery Advertiser*, are real newspapers still published today.

Harper Lee studied law at Alabama State University. A few months after graduating in 1950, she left for New York. She worked as a reservation clerk at an airline for a few years before giving up her job to develop a full-time career as a writer.

Key point

Use an internet search engine like Google (www.google.co.uk) to find appropriate websites about Monroeville, Alabama. Study the sites to get a sense of what the town is like now, and what it was like in the past. The old courthouse, where Harper Lee must have visualised the trial of Tom Robinson, is now a museum.

Slavery

To make sense of *To Kill a Mockingbird*, you need to understand the history of Alabama and the other Southern states.

TopFoto

Black workers gather the cotton harvest in Louisiana

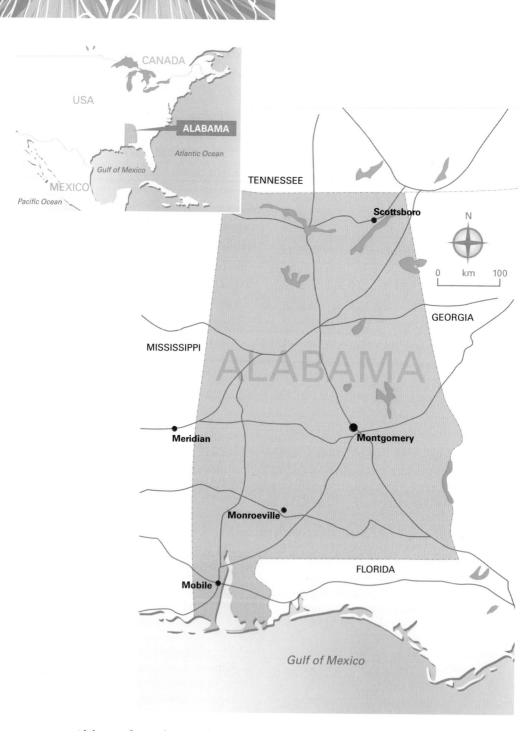

Alabama, formerly an independent state, signed up to become part of the USA in 1819. In the late 1700s and early 1800s, the Southern states had a thriving economy based on the production of cotton and other valuable crops like sugar and rice. Plantations (large farms) were owned by rich white families who ran their businesses by using hundreds of black slaves as their labour force.

These black people, or their ancestors, had been forcibly transported to the Caribbean and to the USA from Africa on the notorious slave ships. Many of the ships involved were owned by British traders who made large profits out of this 'cargo' until slave trading was made illegal in Britain in 1807.

In the Southern states, the slaves picked and processed the crops and did all the menial jobs. They lived in basic accommodation provided on-site by the plantation owner. They were slaves and therefore not free to leave. Only if they were sold did they move. They were not paid for their work but food was provided. A few lucky individuals worked in their owners' homes as domestic servants such as cooks, cleaners and carers of children. These slaves usually lived in a building close to the house or sometimes in servants' rooms within the house.

This system meant that white landowners could afford to live elegantly in large houses. Before 1861, there was a distinctive leisurely, aristocratic lifestyle among slave owners in the unindustrialised Southern states.

Life was different in the industrialised North of the country. Northerners objected to what they saw as the exploitation of black people by their fellow Americans in the South, which, incidentally, gave the South an 'unfair' advantage over the North commercially. Therefore, those in the North campaigned for the abolition of slavery.

The result was that the Southern states, including Alabama, tried to secede (break away) from the Union. They wanted to form a new country called the Confederate States of America. This led to a Civil War between the Northern (Union) states and the Southern (Confederate) states, fought on the issue of slavery, between 1861 and 1865.

The Confederates lost the war. Slavery was outlawed immediately by the Emancipation Proclamation. In practice, however, most slaves continued to work for their former owners on the same plantations and the notion of equal status was a short-lived ideal.

Black people continued to be treated as inferior, made to live separately from whites and denied their rights. They were free in name only for almost another century. *To Kill a Mockingbird* shows blacks, like the Robinsons and the congregation of Calpurnia's church, living apart from the white community and with a poor standard of living 70 years after the Civil War.

The 1930s

The Wall Street Crash of 1929, in which many company shares became worthless overnight, led to a period of poverty and high unemployment throughout the USA and Europe. Wall Street is the street in New York in and around which

Desperate times followed the Wall Street Crash of October 1929

banks and financial institutions are clustered. It is the equivalent of the City district of London.

The situation was worst between 1933 and 1935. This time is known as the Great Depression and Harper Lee, like her creation Scout Finch, grew up during this period. In *To Kill a Mockingbird* the (white) Cunninghams and Ewells, and most of the black people, are poor partly because of the Depression.

The 1930s was a decade of change. In 1931, when Harper Lee was five years old, nine young black men were arrested in Scottsboro, Alabama and tried for the rape of two white women. Just as Tom Robinson is threatened by a lynch mob in *To Kill a Mockingbird*, these men came close to being killed by a vigilante group before trial. Although medical evidence proved that the women had not been raped, the defendants were all found guilty by the all-white jury. They were sentenced to death apart from the youngest, aged only 12. After a series of appeals and retrials, they were eventually proved to be innocent and all but one of them was freed or granted parole.

The miscarriage of justice at Scottsboro, and other similar trials in which people were judged by their colour and not on the facts, obviously influenced Harper Lee. It is not hard to see why she included Tom Robinson's trial as the climax of the plot of *To Kill a Mockingbird*. Her novel is really about the attempt of one man, Atticus Finch, to make his community recognise that black people are full human beings entitled to equal rights.

The 1950s and 1960s

During the 1950s, towns in Alabama and elsewhere in the Southern states were insular and isolated. Racial tension still dominated. Harper Lee, who has always divided her time between Monroeville and New York, would have been well aware of this. Scout describes Maycomb as 'a tired old town' for whose inhabitants there is 'nothing to see outside the boundaries of Maycomb County'.

By 1954, Martin Luther King Jr was working as a Baptist church minister in Montgomery and his civil rights work began there. He worked to bring an end to prejudice and segregation, and to ensure voting rights for black people.

Martin Luther King Jr speaking at a mass rally in Philadelphia

In 1955, Rosa Parks, a black woman, refused to give up her seat to a white man on a bus in Montgomery, leading to a bus boycott by black people that eventually forced the end of segregated public transport. Harper Lee would have been writing her novel at this time. However, it was not until after Martin Luther King Jr's assassination in 1968 that, at last, his life's aims began to be fulfilled.

To Kill a Mockingbird was first published in 1960. It had been reviewed by a publisher three years before in 1957 and then substantially redrafted. It has since sold over 30 million copies worldwide and has won numerous awards, including the Pulitzer Prize. It remains Harper Lee's only novel, although she has written magazine articles and essays. In 1962, it was made into a successful film starring Gregory Peck as Atticus, a performance for which he won an Oscar.

A Southern novel

The Southern states had — and still have — a clear identity of their own. It is possible that this identity was formed or strengthened by their defeat in the American Civil War.

'Southern novels' (novels written by American authors from the South) tend to be regional and to present a strong sense of place. They also convey a feeling of loneliness and isolation. Notice the way Harper Lee describes the layout of Maycomb in such detail that the reader knows where each place is in relation to the rest of the town.

Key point

As a revision or note-making exercise, draw a map of Maycomb as you read the novel.

Danita Delimont/Alamy

The courthouse in Monroeville

After the Civil War, the Southern states went into a long decline and were, in some ways, cut off from the progressive North. Poverty was worse in the South during the Depression than in the North because farming, on which the South depended, was badly affected.

Although many Southerners moved North, this was prompted by and led to ambivalent feelings. The migrants suffered homesickness and nostalgia and regretted the passing of the old Southern traditions. On the other hand, many of them hated the Southern values that had driven them North in the first place. In *To Kill a Mockingbird,* for example, Dolphus Raymond sends his 'mixed' children to the North where they will not stand out as being different.

You can see this ambivalence clearly in the novel. Harper Lee recognises that there is much that is wrong with Maycomb, but she also presents a certain affection for its ways. There is gentle exasperation in telling the reader that 'Maycomb was interested by the news of Tom's death for perhaps two days'.

White Southerners are proud of their aristocratic heritage — look at the discussions about 'fine folks' in *To Kill a Mockingbird* and at the views of Aunt Alexandra (Chapter 13). On the other hand, there is a sense of guilt. Many Maycomb inhabitants are still living mentally in the age of slavery, but characters like Atticus, Miss Maudie and Calpurnia are beginning to prick at other people's consciences. Like many Southern novelists, Harper Lee expresses pride in the South's history alongside shame at its racism.

Violence, often directed at black people, is also typical of Southern novels. The party of Old Sarum men coming in the night to confront the jailed Tom Robinson is firmly in this tradition.

Southern values mean that, however bad things are, you must defend your honour. The Ewells live on a rubbish dump and are, in a sense, worse off than anyone else in the novel. Bob Ewell is a violent liar who lives on state benefits and spends all his money on drink, but he is determined to protect his 'honour'. This attitude is partly rooted in fear. After the abolition of slavery, some white people were afraid they would lose not only land and money but also status.

Key point

Ideas for other Southern fiction you might like to try:

* *The Adventures of Huckleberry Finn* by Mark Twain, 1884

* *Gone with the Wind* by Margaret Mitchell, 1936. Like *To Kill a Mockingbird*, *Gone with the Wind* was an immediate bestseller, winning the Pulitzer Prize and being made into a world-famous film

* *The Little Friend* by Donna Tartt, 2002

* *Roll of Thunder, Hear my Cry* by Mildred E. Taylor, 1976

* *The Sound and the Fury* by William Faulkner, 1929

* *A Tree of Night* and other stories by Truman Capote, 1949

Review your learning

1 Where, when and how did Harper Lee grow up?

2 Why was a Civil War fought in the USA?

3 Who led the US campaign for equal rights for black people in the 1950s and 1960s?

4 How did the Wall Street Crash affect ordinary people?

5 What real incident did Harper Lee base the Robinson rape trial on?

6 What do you understand by the term 'Southern values'?

7 What do Southern novels tend to have in common?

8 In view of what you know about Harper Lee's background, why do you think she wrote *To Kill a Mockingbird*?

9 Why do you think *To Kill a Mockingbird* has been such a successful novel, with high sales worldwide?

Plot and structure

> What happens in each chapter?
> How is the timing of events in the novel worked out?
> What is the overall 'shape' of the novel?
> How does Harper Lee organise her material to keep the reader interested?

Part One

Chapter 1

* We are introduced to the Finch family and their background.
* We learn that Charlie Baker Harris (Dill) is staying next door with Miss Rachel Haverford for the summer.
* The first mention is made of Boo Radley.

Atticus Finch is a widowed lawyer bringing up two children, Jean Louise ('Scout') — who is telling the story — and Jeremy ('Jem'), in Maycomb with the assistance of Calpurnia, a respected black cook, housekeeper and substitute mother. Scout is six years old and Jem four years older. The children make friends with Charles Baker ('Dill') Harris, a visitor from Meridian in Mississippi. He is spending the summer with his aunt. All three children are fascinated by the unseen Arthur ('Boo') Radley, a neighbour who only leaves his house at night. The children play imaginative games influenced by books and films, and Dill is determined to coax Boo Radley out of his house so that they can see what he is really like.

Chapter 2

* Dill leaves Maycomb.
* Scout has her first morning at school.
* Miss Caroline Fisher's teaching methods disappoint Scout.
* Walter Cunningham's poverty causes a misunderstanding at school.

Scout misses Dill and finds school disappointing because her young teacher, who is new to the school, disapproves of her ability to read. Scout has never been taught to read but has absorbed the skill through living in a 'bookish' home. Scout finds the young Miss Caroline's teaching methods restrictive. There is also a misunderstanding when Scout tries to explain to Miss Caroline that Walter Cunningham has brought neither packed lunch nor money to school because he is poor. The teacher tries to lend him money and gets annoyed with Scout, who tries to explain why Walter will not take it. Scout knows the family because, in the previous year, Atticus had done legal work for Walter's father for which Mr Cunningham was unable to pay. Atticus had explained to Scout that his client would pay 'in kind' by bringing, for example, logs and hickory nuts for the Finch family.

Text focus

Look carefully at Chapter 2 from 'My special knowledge of the Cunningham Tribe' to 'Jem's definitions are very nearly accurate sometimes'. Read it several times.

➤ Note that Jem tells Scout that an entailment is 'a condition of having your tail in a crack'. This is an example of one of Harper Lee's many wry jokes, this time at Jem's expense. It is an instance of **irony**. Jem has invented the definition, and an entailment is actually a legal term meaning that there is a limitation on what an owner may do with his property. However, can you see what Atticus means when he says 'Jem's definitions are very nearly accurate sometimes'? Mr Cunningham cannot do what he wants to because of the entailment — like an animal whose tail is trapped. That is what makes Jem's definition ironic.

➤ There is evidence in this passage of the poverty that the working people in Maycomb experience and the reaction of professional people such as lawyers and doctors to it. They will accept goods such as logs, nuts, holly or potatoes as payment for services instead of money. Such bartering of goods and services helps everyone in difficult times because poverty caused by an economic depression affects all classes. Atticus tells Scout, 'We are indeed' when she asks him whether their own family is poor.

➤ Harper Lee often uses short sentences with one subject and one verb, such as 'We watched', 'Jem's nose wrinkled' and 'Entailment was only part of Mr Cunningham's vexations'. The technical name for this is a **simple sentence** (as opposed to a **compound** or **complex sentence**). The frequency of simple sentences makes the writing direct and incisive. It is an appropriate style for a story about children growing up. Find other examples of simple sentences in this passage and think about their effect.

➤ Look carefully at the way Harper Lee sets out the dialogue in this passage. She makes it move quickly by omitting 'he said', 'she said' or their equivalents. It is a technique borrowed from drama and perhaps it is not surprising that the novel

has been made into a successful film and a play for live performance. Lee's style of writing conversations already reads rather like a play script.

* Earlier in this chapter, Scout says, 'He hasn't taught me anything, Miss Caroline. Atticus ain't got time to teach me anything.' What evidence can you find here that shows this is untrue?
* What is the evidence that the Cunninghams are a 'set breed of men'?

Chapter 3

* Jem invites Walter Cunningham to lunch with the Finches.
* Calpurnia rebukes Scout for her bad manners towards Walter.
* We are introduced to the Ewell family through Burris, who is both dirty and rude at school.
* Scout discusses school with Atticus.

Jem invites Walter Cunningham home for lunch where Atticus courteously talks to his visitor about crops in an adult way that his own children do not understand. Scout, on the other hand, comments tactlessly on Walter's eating habits. Calpurnia is angry with Scout for making a visitor feel uncomfortable and threatens her with having to eat in the kitchen in future. In the afternoon, Miss Caroline is upset by filthy Burris Ewell, whose hair is infested with lice and who storms abusively out of school. At home that evening, Scout discusses her day with Atticus and tells him she does not want to go to school. She would rather stay at home as the Ewells do. Atticus explains sympathetically that she does not have a choice and promises to go on reading with her in spite of the teacher's instructions.

Chapter 4

* Scout and Jem find gifts in a tree on the edge of the Radley property.
* Dill returns for summer 1934.
* Atticus questions the children about their make-believe games.
* Scout hears the Radleys laughing.

Scout finds some wrapped chewing gum left for her in a knothole in an oak tree near the Radley house. Later, she and Jem find old coins there. With Dill, they begin to develop a make-believe game based on local rumours and legends about Boo Radley. Atticus catches them and suspects they are planning to torment Boo, but Jem assures him they are not. Scout thinks she hears laughter in the Radley house when she unintentionally gets close to it by rolling inside a tyre that goes its own way and ends up wedged on the Radleys' steps.

Chapter 5

* Miss Maudie explains Boo Radley's background to Scout.
* The children try to provoke Boo Radley into appearing.
* Atticus catches them and forbids them to play 'One Man's Family'.

Miss Maudie Atkinson is a sensible and humane neighbour who dislikes gossip. She tells Scout some of the sad truth about Boo Radley. He is a shy, damaged man bullied by his late father, and he just wants to stay indoors. The next day, Scout persuades the boys to let her play with them and the three children try to entice Boo Radley out of his house by delivering a letter on the end of a fishing rod. Atticus, home by chance to collect some papers, discovers them and stops the game. He forbids them to play the Boo Radley-based make-believe game, having tricked Jem into admitting to what they were doing.

Chapter 6

* The children creep up to the Radley house in the dark.
* Nathan Radley shoots at them and misses.
* Jem leaves his trousers behind.

Partly because it is Dill's last night in Maycomb, the children dare each other to sneak onto the Radley veranda in the dark. Boo's elder brother, Nathan, mistakes them for a black burglar and shoots. He misses. In the panic as they run way, Jem catches his trousers on a wire fence and has to leave them behind. Inevitably, local people hear the noise and come out of their houses to investigate. Dill tells them that Jem has lost his trousers in a game of strip poker. While Scout lies awake and worries, Jem returns to retrieve the trousers later in the night when the commotion has died down.

Pause for thought

How is Harper Lee gradually building up the character of Atticus? Why do you think she gave him the same name as a Roman nobleman and diplomat, Atticus Titus Pomponius (109–32 BC), who was known for his impartial wisdom and interest in books?

Chapter 7

* Jem is surprised to find that someone had repaired his trousers before he retrieved them.
* The children find more items in the tree, first string and sculptures of themselves, then a spelling medal and a pocket watch.
* Nathan Radley blocks up the hole in the tree.

Scout realises that something is upsetting Jem and eventually he tells her that when he went back to the Radley house, his trousers had been mended and deliberately left on the top of the fence for him to collect. In the hole in the oak tree the children find, over several weeks, a ball of string, models of themselves carved in soap, a spelling medal and a watch on a chain. Soon they discover the hole has been filled with cement by Nathan Radley. He pretends it is because the tree is dying. Actually, it is a malicious act to stop his brother leaving things for the children.

Chapter 8

* Mrs Radley dies.
* The first snowfall since the nineteenth century arrives in Maycomb.
* The children build a snowman.
* Miss Maudie's house is destroyed by fire.

Mrs Radley, mother of Nathan and Boo, dies during the winter 'of natural causes'. Neither Scout nor the wider Maycomb community is greatly affected by this news, as Mrs Radley was rarely seen. Scout sees her first snow and is comically frightened until she realises what it is (snow is unusual in Alabama). The children build a snowman to look like their fat neighbour, Mr Avery. During the night, Miss Maudie's house accidentally catches fire and is destroyed, but she shows great courage in accepting the loss. Someone quietly puts a blanket around Scout's shoulders while she is watching the fire and the rest of the neighbourhood is trying to put it out. She only realises that there is a mystery afterwards when she and her family discover that she has possession of a blanket that does not belong to them.

Chapter 9

* We learn that Atticus is to defend a black man accused of rape.
* Scout has already endured taunts at school about her father's tolerant attitude to black people.
* The Finches spend Christmas at Aunt Alexandra's home.
* Scout fights her second cousin Francis.
* Scout is disciplined by Uncle Jack.
* Scout overhears a conversation between Atticus and Uncle Jack.

Cecil Jacobs taunts Scout at school because her 'daddy defended niggers'. When Scout discusses this with Atticus, he explains that he intends to defend Tom Robinson, a black man accused of rape. Atticus is a man of conscience and principle and regards this as something he has to do, although he knows it may make difficulties for his children. Meanwhile, the children and Atticus spend Christmas with Aunt Alexandra, sister to Atticus and Jack. Her grandson Francis, Scout's second cousin, goads Scout about her 'nigger-lover' father, which leads to a fight. Uncle Jack, a doctor, smacks Scout to punish her for fighting and for her abusive language. Later he apologises to her when he learns what the fight was about. At the end of the chapter, Scout overhears a conversation between her father and his brother, which she later realises she was intended to hear. Atticus is telling Jack that he hopes his children will have the sense to go to their father for answers when things are difficult before and during the trial rather than listening to gossip.

Chapter 10

* Atticus gives the children airguns and advice about shooting, although he never shoots.
* A rabid dog appears further down the road.
* Atticus is called home from work.
* A skilled marksman, Atticus kills the dog with a single shot.

The children regard Atticus as 'feeble' because he is 50 years old and never takes part in sports, such as shooting, as other, younger fathers do. He has, however, bought the children airguns. Although he allows them to shoot at birds, Atticus insists that the children 'remember it's a sin to kill a mockingbird', because mockingbirds do no harm — they simply sing. One Saturday the children spot a 'mad', and therefore highly dangerous, dog slowly approaching the house ('mad' in this context means that the dog has rabies). Calpurnia phones Atticus, who comes home immediately with Heck Tate, the sheriff. Mr Tate asks Atticus to kill the dog because of Atticus's superior skill with a gun. Atticus reluctantly takes aim and with great expertise kills the dog instantly. Neither of his children knew he had ever shown any interest in shooting, but they find out afterwards that, when young, he had been nicknamed 'One-Shot Finch'. It is then explained to them that their father has long since given up shooting for sport for moral reasons.

Chapter 11

* Mrs Dubose taunts the children.
* Jem vandalises Mrs Dubose's garden.
* Atticus makes Jem visit Mrs Dubose daily as a punishment.
* Mrs Dubose, a former morphine addict, dies.

When Jem and Scout go to town they pass the property of Mrs Henry Lafayette Dubose, whose 'vicious' habit is to sit on her porch and make aggressive remarks. When she tells the children 'Your father's no better than the niggers and trash he works for!', Jem's control snaps. Later that day, he bursts into Mrs Dubose's front yard while she is not on her porch and breaks every one of the old lady's camellia bushes with Scout's majorette baton, which he then snaps in two. When Atticus finds out, he makes Jem apologise to Mrs Dubose and clear up the mess. Mrs Dubose then tells Jem that she wants him to call daily to read to her. Atticus insists that Jem does this (and Scout goes too), although Mrs Dubose, now bedridden, usually seems to drift off soon after the children's arrival. Later that spring, Mrs Dubose dies and Atticus explains to the children her great courage and determination in overcoming her addiction to morphine, a pain-killing drug, at the end of her life.

Pause for thought

A subheading for Part One of *To Kill a Mockingbird* could be 'Lessons the children learn'. Think carefully and list everything you can think of that Scout, Jem and Dill learn during the first 11 chapters, ranging from small, apparently trivial things, to major lessons in life. It may be a good idea to organise your ideas in a table with three columns, one for each child.

Part Two

Chapter 12

* Scout is lonely because Jem is growing up and seems distant.
* Calpurnia takes the children to her 'black' church in Atticus's absence.
* A collection is taken at church for Tom Robinson's family.
* Aunt Alexandra comes unexpectedly to stay.

Jem is now 12, becoming moody and less inclined to spend time with Scout. Calpurnia tries to comfort her, but tells her this is inevitable as Jem grows up. Atticus is away on business, leaving Calpurnia in charge of the children, so she takes them to First Purchase African M.E. Church, which has an all-black congregation. At the church, Lula, a member of the congregation, tells Calpurnia she should not bring white children, but everyone else makes Scout and Jem welcome. Scout is fascinated by the fact that because few blacks can read hymn books, they have to sing their hymns line by line. Reverend Sykes coaxes a generous donation for Helen Robinson and her children out of the poor congregation. When they arrive home, Aunt Alexandra is waiting determinedly on the porch for them.

Chapter 13

- Aunt Alexandra entertains Maycomb's ladies.
- We learn of Aunt Alexandra's belief in family 'streaks'.
- The Finch family history and Maycomb's social class or 'caste system' are explained by Atticus.
- Atticus's attempts fail to instil unquestioning family pride in his children.

Aunt Alexandra's semi-permanent visit is clearly due to her belief that the children are not being brought up properly. She has strong opinions and prejudices, and socialises with like-minded people in the town. She believes that each family has definite inherited tendencies. Thus 'No Crawford Minds His Own Business, Every Third Merriweather Is Morbid...never take a cheque from a Delafield without a discreet call to the bank' and so on. Although Aunt Alexandra has come to stay with Atticus's agreement, his attitudes are different from his sister's. When she insists that he try to educate his children in family history and the 'gentle breeding' that makes the Finches 'fine folks', Atticus is uncomfortable and unable to do it seriously. The children accept that Aunt Alexandra's arrival is an adult decision but they are mildly resentful.

Chapter 14

- The children hear gossip about the Finch family in town.
- Aunt Alexandra and Atticus disagree about Calpurnia.
- Dill, who has run away from home, is found under Scout's bed.

When the children shop in central Maycomb, they are increasingly aware of growing hostility towards Atticus. Scout has heard the word 'rape' in the town, so she asks Atticus what it means. He gives her a dry, legal definition, which he knows she will not understand. Aunt Alexandra is horrified to discover that the children have been to Calpurnia's church and tells Atticus that the household no longer needs Calpurnia. Scout then overhears a conversation between Atticus and Aunt Alexandra in which he is adamant that 'Calpurnia's not leaving this house until she wants to'. When Scout goes to bed she feels something strange beneath it and mistakes it for a snake. It turns out to be Dill. He has run away from his mother and stepfather because he feels unwanted. Jem tells Atticus (to Scout's annoyance), who supplies food and contacts Dill's family.

Chapter 15

- Atticus arranges for Dill to stay in Maycomb for a week.
- A group of Tom Robinson's sympathisers come to the Finch household to warn Atticus.

* The next day, Jem, Scout and Dill creep to Maycomb jail after dark.
* Atticus 'guards' Tom Robinson.
* A lynch party from Old Sarum demands that Tom is handed over.
* The situation is diffused, and danger overcome, when Scout innocently speaks to Mr Cunningham.

Dill is allowed to stay in Maycomb for a week thanks to tactful intervention by Atticus. This is the weekend before the trial. On Saturday, Sheriff Heck Tate and Link Deas, a humane white farmer, come to warn Atticus that trouble is likely because Tom Robinson is being moved to Maycomb jail from further away. The next day, Atticus calmly goes to the jail to keep watch. Without permission, the three children follow him after dark. They see a group of men from Old Sarum, where the Cunningham family and others live, arrive at the jail to take and lynch Tom. The situation is dangerous, and when Atticus realises the children are present he is worried and tries to send them home. Jem refuses to go. Eventually, Scout speaks politely, naturally and normally to Mr Cunningham, asking about his entailment. Something about the innocence of this seems to remind Mr Cunningham of ordinary human behaviour. He has second thoughts about taking Tom Robinson by force and the lynch party breaks up.

Chapter 16

* Atticus discusses the scene at the jail with the children over breakfast.
* People come from far afield to attend the trial.
* Dolphus Raymond and his 'mixed' family are outside the courthouse.
* Reverend Sykes finds seats for Scout, Jem and Dill in the black people's gallery because the courtroom is full.

Atticus points out that any mob is made up of people — which is why Scout had been able to get through to Mr Cunningham at the jail. He mentions the newspaper editor Mr Underwood's dislike of blacks, which does not affect his sense of justice. Aunt Alexandra reprimands him for speaking like this in front of Calpurnia. To her, Calpurnia is just a black servant. To Atticus (and Scout and Jem), she is part of the family. The trial is about to begin and people flock to it as if it were a holiday outing. Although the children have been forbidden to attend, they go anyway. Outside the courthouse they see Mr Dolphus Raymond, who has a reputation as a heavy drinker. He has married a black woman and fathered a family of 'mixed' children. Discussing this with Jem is part of Scout's education about life. The court is full and the children get in only because Reverend Sykes takes them in with him to sit in the 'coloured balcony'. Judge Taylor is presiding over the court in his own way, outwardly casual, but actually with a firm grip.

Chapter 17

* The children watch the first part of the trial.
* Heck Tate testifies in court to finding Mayella Ewell beaten up.
* In questioning Heck Tate and Bob Ewell, Atticus establishes important evidence: no doctor was called to Mayella Ewell; Mayella Ewell's right eye was injured; Bob Ewell is left-handed.

Heck Tate explains to the court that he was sent for by Bob Ewell, and arrived to find Mayella lying hurt on the floor. Mayella had told the sheriff that Tom Robinson was responsible for injuring and raping her, although there is no medical evidence to support this. Atticus's skilful questioning of Heck Tate eventually establishes that Mayella's eye injury was to the right eye rather than the left. Although it takes Scout a while to understand the significance of this, it is important because a blow from a right-handed man, aimed straight, would normally land on the left of his victim's body. By asking Ewell to sign his name in court, Atticus rather dramatically demonstrates Ewell's left-handedness and, by implication, it is more likely that Ewell injured his daughter himself than that she was attacked by a right-handed person. Ewell's manner in court is unacceptably aggressive and he is reprimanded several times by Judge Taylor.

Chapter 18

* The trial continues.
* Mayella Ewell alleges that Tom Robinson attacked her while he was hired to chop some wood.
* Atticus's questioning highlights Mayella's poverty, loneliness and deprivation.
* There are hints in court that Bob Ewell beats his daughter.
* Tom Robinson has a withered and useless left arm.

Mayella describes in court how she asked Tom Robinson, a black man known to her, onto her premises to break up an unwanted piece of furniture. While he was there, she says, he set upon her, beat her up and 'took advantage' of her. Atticus's questioning draws attention to Mayella's miserable life. She is the eldest of seven motherless children who live in filth and poverty and for whom Mayella is expected to be responsible. She is 19, isolated and unhappy. Mayella nearly admits that her father is violent towards her when he is drunk, but when she realises the way Atticus's questioning is going she draws back from this. At the end of the chapter, Tom Robinson is asked to stand up. A childhood injury in a cotton gin (a machine used to process picked cotton) has made his left arm useless. He would not, therefore, have been able to strike Mayella's right eye. It is also unlikely

that a one-armed man would have been able to overpower a 'strong girl' like Mayella, who claims he pinned her to the ground.

Chapter 19

* Tom Robinson gives evidence.
* Atticus draws attention to Tom's honesty and truthfulness.
* Tom says that Mayella, to his consternation, 'hugged' and 'kissed' him.
* Tom admits sympathy for Mayella.
* Dill is upset and Scout takes him outside to comfort him.

Tom Robinson, who is 25, is shown to be an honest man — when Atticus asks him about a previous conviction for fighting, he admits immediately to it. Jem understands why Atticus brings this up and explains it to Scout. Later in the chapter this 'character reference' is unofficially confirmed by Mr Link Deas, Tom's white employer. Tom's evidence is that, on the day in question, instead of leaving him to do the job in the yard Mayella brought him into the house on a pretence, having sent the Ewell children into town with carefully hoarded money to buy ice creams. She then made sexual advances towards him. Tom did not respond and tried to get away, but at that moment Bob Ewell looked through the window and was furious with his daughter. Tom ran away. Cross-questioned in court by the prosecutor Mr Gilmer, Tom says 'I felt right sorry for her', which prejudices almost all the white listeners in court against him. The chapter ends with Scout comforting Dill, who is moved to tears by events in court.

Text focus

Look carefully at Chapter 19 from, '"Answer the question," said Judge Taylor' to 'Atticus sat down'. Read it several times.

> Tom Robinson speaks in a non-standard English dialect and a broad Southern American accent. To an extent, most of the characters in *To Kill a Mockingbird* do this because, even among educated people, the speech patterns of Alabama and Mississippi are distinctive. This use of **dialect** and **accent** ensures that readers never forget the setting of the action — Lee's novel is firmly rooted in its place and time. Lee's black speakers, however, generally have stronger accents and make more use of dialect than white ones. She uses **phonetic** (as it sounds) spellings such as suh for sir, chillun for children and 'thout bein' for without being.
> When Tom Robinson says 'She hugged me round the waist', he is, by Maycomb standards in the 1930s, alleging something very serious indeed. He is telling the court that he, a black man, was the subject of sexual advances from a white

woman. Lee does not tell the reader in so many words that this allegation caused noise and exclamations from the people present — she leaves it to the reader's imagination. It is implied. All she says is that Judge Taylor uses his gavel and that order is restored. This is a good example of an author drawing the reader in so tightly that she or he does not need to be told certain things. It is highly skilled writing.

- Courtrooms are a bit like theatres and much of what goes on in them is essentially theatrical. Conversations are conducted in front of an audience and sometimes unexpected things happen. Look at the way Lee makes the dialogue run quickly and dramatically as it would in a play. Words fly backwards and forwards like a tennis volley.
- Look at the language Scout uses to describe Tom Robinson's appearance and behaviour in court, such as 'The witness swallowed hard'. Work out what these sentences tell you about Tom Robinson's state of mind. Why does Lee make Scout state these things in such a simple way?
- 'Tom Robinson's manners were as good at Atticus's.' What do you think Scout means by this? The evidence is in the few lines before this statement.
- Decide how effective you find Lee's use of dialect and accent in this scene. How else might she have achieved a similar effect?

Chapter 20

- Dolphus Raymond reveals that he is not an alcoholic.
- Atticus sums up, arguing that Mayella is a victim of her society.
- Atticus insists that Tom's entitlement to justice is the same as a white man's.
- Calpurnia arrives in court.

Outside the court, Scout and Dill talk to Dolphus Raymond. He offers them a drink and it turns out to be Coca-Cola, not whisky, which he carries around with him. He has deliberately allowed rumours to circulate about his drinking because it gives people a reason for his behaviour. He does not mind the children knowing this because he thinks they will understand. Back inside the court, Atticus is summing up the case and asking the jury to return a verdict of not guilty. He feels sorry for Mayella, whose circumstances are so pitiable through no fault of her own, but stresses that Tom's life matters more. He quotes Thomas Jefferson, who 'once said that all men are created equal', and points out that this applies particularly to courts of law, which are 'great levellers'. The children are brought back to earth when Calpurnia walks into court with a note for Atticus and they realise that she has come in search of them.

Chapter 21

* Calpurnia takes the children home for supper.
* Atticus agrees they can return to hear the verdict.
* The jury, having been out for much longer than usual, finds Tom Robinson guilty.
* The black people in the court rise to their feet in respect as Atticus passes by.

The note from Aunt Alexandra that Calpurnia brings to court demands that the children go home, which they do not want to do. Atticus, who had not realised his children had heard the trial from the gallery, compromises by saying that they must go home for supper but that they may return later in the evening to hear the verdict. The jury is out deliberating for a long time and is still out when the children get back to the courthouse. Eventually, the 12 men return to court with a unanimous verdict that Tom Robinson is guilty. Jem is distressed because he had been confident that his father would win the case — although Atticus had known all along that he would not. As Atticus, exhausted, leaves the court alone, everyone in the black people's gallery stands up in silent respect.

Pause for thought

The concept of trial by jury is nearly eight centuries old. It dates back to the Magna Carta of 1215. The Magna Carta was a document that set out an agreement between King John of England and the people, saying that the power of the king would be reduced and that a parliament would be established. The original document is on display at the British Library in London. When the early settlers arrived in America from England in the sixteenth and seventeenth centuries, they took the principle of trial by jury with them. Having now read Harper Lee's story of Tom Robinson's trial, based on real 1920s and 1930s cases, how fair do you think it was? Would a trial in twenty-first century Britain be fairer? If so, why? Attitudes to trial by jury are beginning to change in Britain. Find out more about proposed changes and work out what you think about them.

Chapter 22

* Jem and Aunt Alexandra are both distressed by the verdict.
* Atticus is planning an appeal.
* Grateful black people send gifts to Atticus.
* Bob Ewell spits at Atticus and swears revenge.

Jem weeps in distress because 'It ain't right'. When the children arrive home with Atticus, they find Aunt Alexandra softer than usual. She also feels justice has not been done and she sympathises with Atticus. The next morning, Atticus is more cheerful and less tired and begins to talk about an appeal against the verdict. Meanwhile, large piles of food are quietly delivered to the house — gifts from black people who want to thank Atticus for his willingness to stand up in public for equal rights and justice. This moves him to tears and temporary speechlessness. At the end of the chapter, Miss Stephanie Crawford and Miss Rachel Haverford report to the children that Bob Ewell has spat in Atticus's face in the post office before witnesses and promised to 'get him'.

Chapter 23

* Atticus is relaxed about Bob Ewell's threat and reassures the children.
* Atticus talks about the law and evidence.
* Aunt Alexandra argues for class distinction and condemns the Cunninghams as 'trash'.
* Jem realises that Boo Radley chooses not to leave his house.

Atticus reasons that Bob Ewell's gesture was just getting his anger 'all out of his system' and reassures the children that they have nothing to fear. Aunt Alexandra disagrees. Atticus discusses rape law and the bringing of evidence at some length with Jem and Scout. He assures Scout that 'We've got a good chance' of either winning on appeal or of persuading the Governor of Alabama to commute the death sentence. He tells the children that, interestingly, it was 'one of your Old Sarum friends' who argued against the other jury members and delayed the final guilty decision. Scout then wants to invite Walter Cunningham to the house again and is firmly told by Aunt Alexandra that she may not because the Cunninghams may be good folks, 'But they're not our kind of folks'. Jem is beginning to understand this in a way that Scout, still only eight, does not. Jem tells her that he thinks Boo Radley stays indoors because he wants to.

Chapter 24

* The Missionary Society meets at the Finches house.
* Scout has to wear a dress and Calpurnia serves cakes.
* The ladies want to help black people in Africa but do not notice the plight of the blacks in Maycomb.
* Atticus takes Calpurnia with him to tell Helen Robinson that Tom is dead.

Scout, the tomboy who habitually wears dungarees ('britches'), is forced into a dress and made to attend a meeting of the Missionary Society because Aunt Alexandra wants her to develop into a 'lady'. The women at the meeting are highly hypocritical, although they do not realise it. They want to help the people of the Mruna tribe in Africa but are insensitively critical of the black people they see every

day. Mrs Merriweather has firm views on how to deal with a 'sulky darky' in your kitchen. She tells Scout to be thankful she lives 'in a Christian home with Christian folks in a Christian town'. Then Atticus arrives home unexpectedly and interrupts the meeting. Tom Robinson has been shot dead while trying to escape from prison. Atticus asks Calpurnia to help him break the news to Tom's widow, Helen.

Chapter 25

- Jem tells Scout to put a harmless insect outside rather than kill it.
- Dill describes the scene when Helen Robinson is told about Tom's death.
- Mr Underwood reports the death in the *Maycomb Tribune*.

There is a 'roly-poly' in the house under Scout's bed. Jem insists that she take it outside and release it safely because 'they don't bother you'. Jem and Dill accompany Atticus and Calpurnia to the Robinson house and Scout recounts the story as it has been told to her by Dill. Helen Robinson is so shocked when she hears the news that she faints. Interest in Tom's death is short-lived in Maycomb, but there is a forceful editorial by Mr Underwood in that week's *Maycomb Tribune*. He likens Tom's death to the 'senseless slaughter of songbirds by hunters and children' (or the slaughter of harmless insects, hence the point of the opening of this chapter).

Chapter 26

- School starts in autumn 1935.
- Scout and Jem pass the Radley house daily and Scout remembers their games of two years before.
- Miss Gates teaches Scout's class about Adolf Hitler and democracy.
- Jem is unaccountably irritable.

Dill has returned to Mississippi for the new school term. Scout and Jem pass the Radley house on the way to school each day. Scout thinks about their old games, longs to see and talk to Boo and, with hindsight, understands that back in 1933 Atticus had known much more about the children's Boo-related activities than he revealed. At school, a current events lesson leads to a discussion about Adolf Hitler's treatment of Jews in Germany. Miss Gates informs the class that Hitler is behaving as he is because Germany is a dictatorship. America, in contrast, is a democracy where, she implies, such things could never happen. At home, Scout tries to talk to Jem about these things but he shouts her down because he does not want to think about it. Atticus comforts her and tries to explain Jem's mixed feelings.

Chapter 27

* Bob Ewell gets a government job but is sacked for laziness.
* Ewell attempts to break into Judge Taylor's house.
* Ewell harasses Helen Robinson until he is stopped by Link Deas.
* Maycomb plans a Halloween pageant.
* Scout is to play the part of a piece of pork.

Maycomb is getting back to normal. Bob Ewell is given a government job, but loses it almost immediately because of his unwillingness to work properly. Someone tries to break into Judge Taylor's house one Sunday evening while the judge is reading. There is an assumption that Bob Ewell is the culprit. Link Deas has created a job for Helen Robinson because he feels sorry for her. Her route to work passes the Ewell house at the rubbish dump unless she walks a mile out of her way. When Link Deas realises that Helen has been subjected to threats and nastiness, he confronts Bob Ewell and stops it. Aunt Alexandra sees all these developments as ominous. Meanwhile, the adults in Maycomb are planning a large-scale pageant for Halloween at the end of October. They want to prevent a recurrence of a children's joke played the previous year on two elderly ladies. The focus of the pageant is on local farmers' produce, so Scout is chosen for the unglamorous role of a piece of meat.

Chapter 28

* Scout and Jem chat about their old childish games.
* At the pageant, Scout falls asleep, misses a cue and feels silly.
* Scout and Jem walk home alone with Scout still in her costume. They are followed and attacked.
* Someone carries Jem, injured and unconscious, into the house.
* Heck Tate tells them that Bob Ewell is dead.

On their way to the pageant, Scout and Jem chat over old times and laugh at their former childishness. At school, Scout, as a performer, goes off with Cecil Jacobs and Jem sits in the audience. Scout makes herself look foolish by falling asleep and missing her cue, so she does not want to see anyone. She and Jem wait until the crowd has dispersed before setting off for home on a quiet path through the trees. Scout keeps her costume on. She hears a voice, then rustling, breathing and footsteps, but assumes it is Cecil Jacobs playing tricks as he had done earlier in the evening. Suddenly the children are attacked by an unidentified assailant. Jem is injured but Scout is protected by the chicken-wire costume. A man picks up Jem, who is unconscious, and carries him the last few yards home. Scout follows, noting

that Jem's arm is broken. Atticus and Aunt Alexandra telephone immediately for Dr Reynolds and Heck Tate. There is an unknown man standing quietly in the corner of Jem's bedroom when Heck Tate informs them that Bob Ewell has been stabbed and is lying dead beneath a tree.

Chapter 29

* Aunt Alexandra is distressed.
* Scout tells Heck Tate about the attack.
* Scout's costume has saved her life.
* Scout realises their unknown rescuer is Boo Radley.

Everyone remains in Jem's bedroom except Aunt Alexandra, who thinks the attack could be her fault because she should not have allowed the children to go out alone when she was so uneasy. She goes to her own room. Scout tells Heck Tate as much as she can about the attack. Atticus explains about Scout's costume, which was badly crushed when she reached home. Heck Tate believes it saved her life. There are marks on Ewell's body caused by the wire of the costume. Suddenly, Scout looks at the pale, thin, silent man in the corner and realises who he must be. 'Hey, Boo,' she says to him.

Chapter 30

* Scout is surprised that the others know Boo.
* Atticus is considerate towards Boo.
* Atticus thinks Jem killed Ewell and that there must be honesty.
* Heck makes Atticus understand that Boo killed Ewell.
* Heck insists that Boo will be protected by a lie.

Atticus gently corrects Scout's manners. She must address the visitor as Mr Arthur. Scout then realises that her father, Dr Reynolds and Heck all know Boo, whom Atticus treats with his usual courtesy and gentleness. Scout is surprised that, for the adults, Boo has never been a mystery figure. Atticus kindly takes Boo outside to the porch and Scout finds him a dark corner where he will be comfortable. Atticus is convinced that Jem killed Ewell in self-defence and that all the normal processes of the law must be observed. He insists that there will be no cover-up. Heck disagrees. Eventually, he gets Atticus to see that he is not trying to protect Jem. It was Boo who killed Ewell and Boo who must be protected. They will say that Ewell fell on his knife and killed himself. Atticus is eventually persuaded, although he is troubled about concealing the truth.

Chapter 31

* Scout takes Boo to say goodnight to Jem.
* Scout walks home with Boo.
* Standing on the Radley porch, she sees the street from Boo's point of view.
* Back at home, she falls asleep while Atticus is reading to her.
* Atticus puts Scout to bed.

Boo is led by Scout to Jem's bedroom to bid the sedated boy good night and is encouraged by Scout to stroke Jem when he seems reluctant to do so. Childlike, he then asks Scout to take him home, which Scout does — in such a way that anyone seeing them would assume Boo was escorting her, not the other way round. She feels sad when Boo goes inside because she wishes she and Jem could have offered Boo the same sort of neighbourly gifts he has given them. Scout returns home, where Atticus is sitting at Jem's bedside quietly reading a book of Jem's to himself. Scout asks him to read *The Grey Ghost* aloud to her. Atticus does this but she soon falls asleep. When Atticus is putting her to bed, Scout tells him she has heard the whole story — about a misunderstood boy who turned out to be 'real nice'.

Pause for thought

Is it ever right to tell a lie? Atticus's whole professional and personal life has been built on telling the truth. Is he right to depart from that now? Scout tells us that he 'sat looking at the floor for a long time'. Then he says to his daughter, 'Mr Ewell fell on his knife. Can you possibly understand?' Does she? Does the reader?

Timeline

Year	Time of year	Chapter	What happens
	Part One		
1933	Early summer	1	The main characters are introduced. Scout is six
	September	2	Dill leaves Maycomb. Scout starts school. Description of the Cunninghams
	September	3	Description of the Ewells
1934	Spring/early summer	4	The children are intrigued by Boo Radley, who leaves gifts in a tree. Dill returns to Maycomb
	Spring/early summer	5	The children try to entice Boo outside by delivering a letter
	Late summer	6	The children creep up to the Radleys' house
	October/November	7	Boo leaves more gifts in the tree before Nathan blocks the hole
	Winter	8	Snowfall in Maycomb. Miss Maudie's fire
	Christmas	9	Atticus agrees to defend Tom Robinson. Christmas at Aunt Alexandra's
1935	February	10	Atticus shoots a rabid dog
	Spring	11	Jem destroys Mrs Dubose's camellias and has to read to her. Mrs Dubose dies
	Part Two		
1935	Summer	12	The children are taken to First Purchase Church by Calpurnia. Aunt Alexandra arrives
	Summer	13	Aunt Alexandra entertains Maycomb's ladies
	Summer	14	Dill returns to Maycomb
	Summer	15	The lynch mob from Old Sarum tries to take Tom from jail. Scout talks to Mr Cunningham

Year	Time of year	Chapter	What happens
1935	Summer	16	The trial starts. The children sit in the black people's gallery
	Summer	17	Heck Tate and Bob Ewell testify
	Summer	18	Mayella Ewell testifies
	Summer	19	Tom Robinson gives evidence
	Summer	20	Scout and Dill learn the truth about Dolphus Raymond
	Summer	21	The jury finds Tom Robinson guilty
	Summer	22	Jem is upset by the verdict. The black community sends gifts to Atticus. Bob Ewell spits at Atticus and vows revenge
	Summer	23	Atticus is relaxed about Bob Ewell's threat
	August	24	Tom tries to escape from jail and is shot dead
	September	25	Dill describes how Helen Robinson is told of Tom's death
	September	26	School starts. Miss Gates teaches about Hitler and the Jews
	October	27	Bob Ewell attempts revenge on Judge Taylor and Helen Robinson. A pageant is planned
	October	28	Scout prepares for the pageant. Scout and Jem are attacked by Bob Ewell. Boo saves them by stabbing Ewell
	October	29	Boo is revealed as the children's saviour
	October	30	Atticus thinks Jem has killed Bob Ewell. Heck Tate proves it was Boo
	October	31	Boo and Scout visit Jem. Scout takes Boo home

Structure

Harper Lee divided *To Kill a Mockingbird* into two parts, Chapters 1–11 form the first part and Chapters 12–31 the second part.

Part One ends with the death of Mrs Dubose and Jem's reaction to it. Jem is still a young boy who 'buried his face in Atticus's shirt front'.

The opening of Part Two finds Jem, now 12, 'difficult to live with, inconsistent, moody'. Scout is puzzled that 'This change in Jem had come about in a matter of weeks' and Calpurnia wisely tells her 'I just can't help it if Mister Jem's growin' up...so you come right on in the kitchen when you feel lonesome. We'll find lots of things to do in here'. By changing the atmosphere between Scout and Jem, Harper Lee is moving the novel into another, more adult, mood for Part Two.

Key point

To Kill a Mockingbird is a carefully structured novel.

Pause for thought

What exactly do the children learn in Part One? Make a detailed list. The obvious starting points are what they learn from their encounters with Boo Radley, Mrs Dubose and Walter Cunningham and what Atticus teaches them, but there are several others. If you include page and chapter references, this will form a useful part of your revision notes.

Key point

The pace of *To Kill a Mockingbird* varies.

Part One shows the three children — Scout, Jem and Dill — learning lessons about life and people. Part Two deals with the lead-up to the trial, the trial itself and its aftermath.

Harper Lee could potentially have divided her novel into three sections, with two sections being made out of Part Two. There is a natural break at the end of Chapter 21 when the trial ends. This is also one of the most dramatic and moving moments in the novel as the jury members say 'Guilty...guilty...guilty' and Scout notices Jem, whose 'hands were white from gripping the balcony rail, and his shoulders jerked as if each "guilty" was a separate stab between them'. The chapter ends with all the black people in the gallery rising to their feet in a powerful gesture of silent respect because, as Reverend Sykes tells Scout, 'Your father's passin'.

The central section of *To Kill a Mockingbird* takes place over a short period of time. Harper Lee makes it more exciting by quickening the pace. Everything that happens occurs within a few weeks during the summer of 1935. This is in contrast to Part One, the main events of which are spread over nearly two years.

After the trial, the action slows again with the last events of the novel spread over about three months. However, remember that, although the trial of Tom Robinson is the central climax of the novel, 'our longest journey together', in which

Jem is seriously injured by Bob Ewell, comes in Chapter 28. This episode forms another climax and one that directly affects the children and Atticus.

This is an unusual structure because in most novels the main climax comes near the end. Here it's as if the second, or subsidiary, climax has bounced off the first. Bob Ewell is trying to get his revenge for what he regards as Atticus's betrayal in court. The irony is that justice was not done in the court of law, but Lee wants the reader to agree that moral justice is done in the woods in Chapter 28.

Harper Lee is skilled in maintaining her reader's interest. Notice, for example, how she brings the children out of the court in Chapter 20 for their talk with Dolphus Raymond. As you read it, you wonder what is happening inside the courtroom. It is a way of heightening the suspense. Something similar happens in Chapter 21 when the jury is 'out' coming to its conclusion and Calpurnia insists on taking the children home for supper. We are left, like Scout, desperate to get back to the court.

Look at the introduction of Boo Radley as a flesh-and-blood human being in Chapter 29. This is the first, and only, time we 'meet' him. Before this he is a shadowy figure who leaves little gifts (Chapters 4 and 7), repairs torn trousers (Chapter 7), or who puts a protective blanket round a child's shoulders (Chapter 8). Scout mistakes him for 'some countryman I did not know' and, for a while, the reader is taken in too. It is not until the end of Chapter 29, where Lee allows Scout three full and detailed paragraphs to describe the pale and troubled Boo, that we realise who Jem's rescuer is. Lee springs this surprise with great skill.

Pause for thought

Make a list of other places in the novel where Harper Lee temporarily holds back the story in order to make the reader wonder. Be sure to include page and chapter references. These will be a useful part of your revision notes.

Review your learning

1 Who says 'Arthur Radley just stays in the house, that's all'?
2 What is the name of:
   a Aunt Alexandra's husband?
   b their grandson?
3 Who gives Helen Robinson a job after Tom's death?
4 Why are 'many phone calls and much pleading on behalf of the defendant' needed and who is the defendant?
5 What does Reverend Sykes make his people do at the end of Chapter 21? Explain why.
6 *To Kill a Mockingbird* is told in 31 chapters. Where are the main events and turning points?
7 What do you regard as the climax of *To Kill a Mockingbird*?

Characterisation

> Who are the characters?
> What are they like?
> How does Harper Lee present them?
> How do the characters relate to each other?
> What part do they play in the plot?
> How do they fit into the novel's themes and ideas?

Jean Louise ('Scout') Finch

Scout says

* 'I was far too old and too big for such childish things, and the sooner I learned to hold in, the better off everybody would be. I soon forgot. Cecil Jacobs made me forget.' (Chapter 9)
* 'Atticus, are we going to win it [the court case]?' (Chapter 9)
* 'Don't you remember me, Mr Cunningham? I'm Jean Louise Finch.' (Chapter 15)
* 'I think there's just one kind of folks. Folks.' (Chapter 23)
* 'Hey, Boo.' (Chapter 29)

Scout

* narrates the story
* can read, so is frustrated by school
* fights against injustice with her fists until she learns self-control
* is curious — although increasingly sympathetic — about Boo Radley
* likes to play with her elder brother and not to be left out
* resents her Aunt Alexandra and sometimes Calpurnia
* admires, loves and respects her father
* visits Calpurnia's church
* attends the trial of Tom Robinson
* takes part in a pageant at school
* is there when Jem is injured by Bob Ewell, who is then killed by Boo Radley

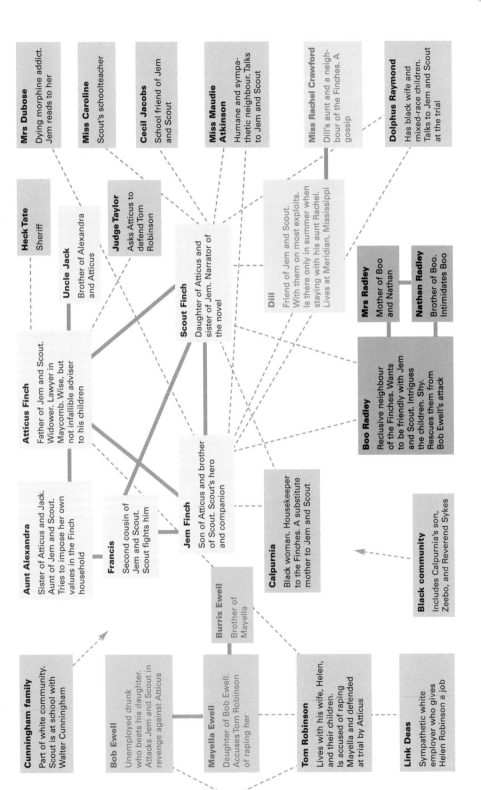

Mrs Dubose
Dying morphine addict. Jem reads to her

Miss Caroline
Scout's schoolteacher

Cecil Jacobs
School friend of Jem and Scout

Miss Maudie Atkinson
Humane and sympathetic neighbour. Talks to Jem and Scout

Miss Rachel Crawford
Dill's aunt and a neighbour of the Finches. A gossip

Dolphus Raymond
Has black wife and mixed-race children. Talks to Jem and Scout at the trial

Heck Tate
Sheriff

Uncle Jack
Brother of Alexandra and Atticus

Judge Taylor
Asks Atticus to defend Tom Robinson

Atticus Finch
Father of Jem and Scout. Widower. Lawyer in Maycomb. Wise, but not infallible adviser to his children

Scout Finch
Daughter of Atticus and sister of Jem. Narrator of the novel

Dill
Friend of Jem and Scout. With them on most exploits. Is there only in summer when staying with his aunt Rachel. Lives at Meridian, Mississippi

Mrs Radley
Mother of Boo and Nathan

Nathan Radley
Brother of Boo. Intimidates Boo

Boo Radley
Reclusive neighbour of the Finches. Wants to be friendly with Jem and Scout. Intrigues the children. Shy. Rescues them from Bob Ewell's attack

Aunt Alexandra
Sister of Atticus and Jack. Aunt of Jem and Scout. Tries to impose her own values in the Finch household

Francis
Second cousin of Jem and Scout. Scout fights him

Jem Finch
Son of Atticus and brother of Scout. Scout's hero and companion

Calpurnia
Black woman. Housekeeper to the Finches. A substitute mother to Jem and Scout

Black community
Includes Calpurnia's son, Zeebo, and Reverend Sykes

Cunningham family
Part of white community. Scout is at school with Walter Cunningham

Bob Ewell
Unemployed drunk who beats his daughter. Attacks Jem and Scout in revenge against Atticus

Burris Ewell
Brother of Mayella

Mayella Ewell
Daughter of Bob Ewell. Accuses Tom Robinson of raping her

Tom Robinson
Lives with his wife, Helen, and their children. Is accused of raping Mayella and defended at trial by Atticus

Link Deas
Sympathetic white employer who gives Helen Robinson a job

Character chart for *To Kill a Mockingbird*
Unbroken lines indicate family relationships

Scout thinks that

* every human being should be taken at face value irrespective of skin colour or social class
* Atticus is an almost infallible source of wisdom and guidance
* Jem, Calpurnia and Miss Maudie all know things that she does not
* Tom Robinson is the victim of terrible injustice

Harper Lee presents Scout

* entirely through the character's own words
* by sometimes letting us see 'past' Scout to reveal the way she is seen by other characters
* by showing us Scout in a variety of situations

Conclusions

Scout is six when the novel opens and nine when it ends. She is the younger child and only daughter of Atticus Finch, a widowed lawyer. She is the narrator, so everything is seen from her point of view. However, the story is being told by the adult Scout in the 1950s. She is looking back and remembering the events of 1933–35, 'when enough years had gone by to enable us to look back,' she says on the first page, although we never 'meet' the adult Scout. It is as if the novel is a memoir, and we learn about Scout's character from every word because we see everything from her point of view. She is the novel's central and most important character.

This technique means that the narrator uses adult language and interprets as an adult the events she is describing. It is a slightly humorous adult voice, for example, which says 'I mumbled that I was sorry and retired meditating upon my crime. I never deliberately learned to read, but somehow I had been wallowing illicitly in daily papers' (Chapter 2).

Scout is a sensitive girl. Look at the way she speaks to Mr Cunningham at the jail in Chapter 15 and at how gently she speaks to Boo Radley in Chapter 30. She is also intelligent. 'Scout yonder's been readin' ever since she was born,' Jem tells Dill in Chapter 1. Most of the time she keeps up with Jem, who is four years her senior, and Atticus habitually addresses her as if she were almost adult: 'This case, Tom Robinson's case, is something that goes to the essence of a man's conscience' (Chapter 11). That is why school is such a disappointment to her. She is already ahead of what it can offer and she predicts, probably accurately, that she has 'twelve years of unrelieved boredom' ahead of her (Chapter 4).

Scout's affectionate nature is obvious in the way she relates to Atticus and Calpurnia. She adores Jem who, as her older brother, has almost the status of a hero in her life. Look at Chapter 6 when Jem returns to collect his trousers from the Radley house and Scout cannot sleep for worrying about him. It is an example of how close she is to him. She also devotedly accompanies him to Mrs Dubose's house in Chapter 11. Notice too how attached she is to Dill: 'With him, life was routine; without him, life was unbearable,' she remarks in Chapter 12.

She is not 'ladylike' and almost always wears dungarees ('britches' or 'overalls'). This is partly because her mother died when she was two and her main role models have been Atticus and Jem. Aunt Alexandra ('Enamoured, upright, uncompromising', Chapter 12) is critical of both Scout's tomboy nature and Atticus's parenting skills. This causes tension when Aunt Alexandra first comes to stay, although Scout's respect for her grows as time goes on. Scout is more comfortable with male companions like Atticus, Jem and Dill because they are more open with each other than her aunt's 'sipping, whispering, fanning' friends who call in the afternoons when Scout is usually 'mud-splashed or covered with sand' (Chapter 13).

Scout is a fully rounded and believable character, which is one of the factors that makes *To Kill a Mockingbird* a compelling novel. As well as being thoughtful and perceptive, she is impulsive and has a fiery temper. Look at the way she gets into fights with Walter Cunningham (Chapter 3) and Cecil Jacobs (Chapter 9) when she forgets Atticus's stern advice about fighting. Cecil Jacobs has been taunting her, saying that 'Scout Finch's daddy defended niggers'. She also fights her insufferable second cousin Francis (Chapter 9) because he calls her father a 'nigger-lover' and there is a fight with Jem in Chapter 14. Nevertheless she eventually follows Atticus's advice to fight with her head. At the end of the novel, the more mature nine-year-old Scout, having learned the lessons of Tom Robinson's trial, Bob Ewell's death and the truth about Boo Radley, is — the reader senses — much less likely to get involved in fist fighting.

Scout believes that Atticus is an almost infallible source of wisdom and guidance

The key advice Atticus offers his children is that they must learn to get inside another person's skin and walk around in it. At first, Scout responds emotionally to what happens to her. On the first day at school, she is sorry for Walter Cunningham. Then she fights him, and treats him discourteously when Jem invites him home for lunch. She is reacting with her heart rather than her head. At the end of the novel, Scout is able to empathise with Boo Radley, Aunt Alexandra and Mayella Ewell. She has learned to use her head ('It's a good one, even if it does

resist learning' Atticus tells her teasingly in Chapter 9) to imagine how things seem from other people's points of view.

Scout has no prejudices, so she contrasts with characters in the novel such as Bob Ewell, Nathan Radley, Miss Stephanie Crawford and the Cunninghams. She is a child, with a child's approach to life and a child's mind, so she sees things as they are. In Scout's opinion, Calpurnia, Tom Robinson and the rest of the black community are simply human beings and she makes no distinction: there is 'just one kind of folks. Folks' (Chapter 23).

Atticus Finch

Atticus says

* 'You never really understand a person until you consider things from his point of view — until you climb into his skin and walk around in it.' (Chapter 3)
* 'it's a sin to kill a mockingbird' (Chapter 10)
* 'before I can live with other folks I've got to live with myself. The one thing that doesn't abide by majority rule is a person's conscience' (Chapter 11)
* 'It's not okay to hate anybody.' (Chapter 26)

Gregory Peck as Atticus Finch

Atticus

* defends Tom Robinson on a charge of rape
* shoots a rabid dog
* talks patiently to his children
* is always courteous
* underestimates Bob Ewell
* is highly respected by most Maycomb people

Atticus thinks that

* humans can live peacefully together only if they empathise with each other
* tolerance is essential
* for a Christian, the teaching of Christ underpins every attitude and action
* all races should be treated equally

Harper Lee presents Atticus

* through Scout's point of view, so we see intimate moments in family life
* in court

* relating to the residents of Maycomb, such as Miss Maudie, Heck Tate and Mr Underwood
* as treating Calpurnia with courtesy and respect
* as teaching his children how to behave by example

Conclusions

Atticus Finch, 50, belongs to an old Maycomb family descended from Simon Finch, an early settler. The family owns land at Finch's Landing, but Atticus is the first Finch to have become a lawyer. He practises in the town of Maycomb and, because he has been a widower for four years at the opening of the novel, is bringing up his children Jem and Scout alone with the assistance of a black house-keeper, Calpurnia.

He is asked by Judge Taylor to take on the Tom Robinson rape case because only Atticus would make a serious attempt to defend a black man. Although Atticus knows his children will suffer taunts because of it, he believes he must take on the case. To him, it is a matter of conscience and self-respect. 'If I didn't I couldn't hold up my head in town, I couldn't represent the county in the legislature, I couldn't even tell you or Jem not to do something again,' he tells Scout in Chapter 9, adding that 'every lawyer gets at least one case in his lifetime that affects him personally. This one's mine, I guess.'

> **Pause for thought**
>
> Gregory Peck won an Oscar for his portrayal of Atticus in the 1962 film of *To Kill a Mockingbird*. Watch the film carefully and critically. What aspects of Atticus's character does Peck bring out well? How far do you think Peck's performance accurately depicts the Atticus you know from your reading?

Atticus stands for Christian values. He tries to practise forgiveness and tolerance. Look, for example, at the way he behaves to Mrs Dubose in Chapter 11, despite the fact that she has said some malicious things about him and has immaturely distressed his children. Christianity teaches 'Love thy neighbour as thyself' (Matthew 19:19) and 'turn the other cheek' (Matthew 5:39), and that is what Atticus tries to do with everyone he meets. Harper Lee contrasts his attitude with the hypocritical Christians in the novel, such as the ladies at Aunt Alexandra's Missionary Society in Chapter 24. Mrs Merriweather tells Scout she lives 'in a Christian home with Christian folks in a Christian town'. Harper Lee means the reader to smile at the irony of this. The ladies want to help the black people of the distant Mruna tribe. Yet Mrs Merriweather, who cannot stand a 'sulky darky' in her kitchen and tells her servant to copy Jesus and complain less, cannot see that her dismissive attitude towards Maycomb's black community is profoundly un-Christian.

Atticus is a conscientious father who always makes time to talk to his children: 'he played with us, read to us, and treated us with courteous detachment,' Scout says in Chapter 1. His parenting skills are contrasted in the novel with those of Mr Radley, Bob Ewell and — more distantly — Dill's parents. Whenever Scout is miserable or puzzled, she turns to Atticus and he is always available. In Chapter 11, for example, Scout is annoyed with Atticus for sending Jem to apologise to Mrs Dubose, but she ends up in his arms being reassured. The way he tucks her comfortably into bed at the end of the novel is another example of his constantly reassuring stance.

Atticus also disciplines his children firmly when he thinks it is necessary. He stops them playing 'One Man's Family' in Chapter 4 and insists they leave the court to have supper at home with Calpurnia in Chapter 21. Unfailingly courteous himself, he even gently corrects Scout in Chapter 30 for her over-familiarity in addressing Boo Radley as 'Boo' instead of the more polite 'Mr Arthur'.

However, Atticus also makes mistakes as a father. He underestimates the seriousness of Bob Ewell's threats after the trial and exposes his children to serious risk as a result. 'We don't have anything to fear from Bob Ewell, he got it all out of his system that morning,' he tells Jem and Scout after being spat at in the post office (Chapter 23). In Chapter 28, Jem and Scout are attacked by the vengeful Mr Ewell. Jem's arm is badly broken and Scout is saved from injury or death only by her bulky, wire-framed pageant costume. In this case, Aunt Alexandra is more perceptive than her brother. In Chapter 23 she observes that 'His kind'd do anything to pay off a grudge' and warns Atticus to expect 'something furtive'.

Atticus, who has the respect of decent citizens such as Miss Maudie, Heck Tate, Judge Taylor, Calpurnia and Reverend Sykes, is 'civilised in his heart' (Chapter 10). He is presented as an embodiment of everything Harper Lee respects in a lawyer, citizen, Christian and father. He is the moral centre of *To Kill a Mockingbird*.

Jeremy ('Jem') Finch

Jem says

- [of Boo] 'Ain't scared, just respectful' (Chapter 1)
- [at Calpurnia's church] 'Let's go home, Cal, they don't want us here' (Chapter 12)
- 'around here once you have a drop of Negro blood, that makes you all black' (Chapter 16)
- 'don't fret, we've won it [the court case]...Don't see how any jury could convict on what we heard' (Chapter 21)
- 'If there's just one kind of folks, why can't they get along with each other? If

Jem and Scout Finch (Philip Alford and Mary Badham)

Universal/The Kobal Collection

they're all alike, why do they go out of their way to despise each other?' (Chapter 23)

* 'Run, Scout! Run! Run!' (Chapter 28)

Jem

* is intensely and childishly curious about Boo Radley at the beginning of the novel
* loses his temper and vandalises Mrs Dubose's camellias
* provides a commentary on the trial for Scout and the reader
* is injured in the attack by Bob Ewell
* is a silent (sleeping) presence in the final scenes of the novel
* is nearly always with Scout

Jem thinks that

* all races should have equal rights
* Boo Radley is a reclusive monster, until he eventually works out that Boo remains in the house simply because he wants to stay inside

- Mrs Dubose is a spiteful old woman, until, with Atticus's help, he learns to climb into her shoes and walk around in them
- Tom Robinson will get justice because of Atticus's fine advocacy, but he is wrong
- he and Scout will be safe walking home from the pageant but, again, he is wrong

Harper Lee presents Jem

- through Scout's point of view so that we see him as an older brother — sometimes wise, occasionally exasperating, often pretending to know more than he does, usually dependable
- as intelligent, perceptive and deeply interested in Atticus's work — it is not hard to foresee Jem's likely later profession
- in a range of situations, such as retrieving his trousers from the Radley house, reading aloud to Mrs Dubose and trying to protect Scout from serious danger after the pageant

Conclusions

Jem Finch is four years older than Scout, so he moves from being a child of nearly ten to a thoughtful adolescent of about 13 during the course of *To Kill a Mockingbird*. As Scout's elder brother, he is expected to look after her and he often tells her things she (and the reader) would not otherwise know. Jem, for example, can remember their dead mother but Scout cannot (Chapter 1). Chapter 7 finds Jem assuring Scout that 'the older [she] got the better school would be'. In Chapter 14, when Jem takes Scout to his room because Atticus and Aunt Alexandra are 'fussing' (quarrelling), he tells her that Atticus has 'a lot on his mind now' and that 'It's this Tom Robinson case that's worryin' him to death'. Scout comments on his 'maddening superiority' and says she finds it 'unbearable'. She shouts at him: 'Jee-crawling-hova, Jem! Who do you think you are?' Irritating as it might be to Scout, it is a sign that Jem is growing up fast.

Pause for thought

In what ways do you think Jem and Atticus are alike? How does Harper Lee achieve this resemblance, considering their physical differences? How difficult do you think it is for a novelist to convey in writing family likenesses of manner and attitude?

Of all the characters in the novel, Jem is perhaps the one who changes most. At the beginning he is a young boy who spends hours playing childish games with Scout and Dill, mainly focusing on the rather unkind curiosity about Boo Radley that obsesses all three children. By the end of the novel, he is a teenager lying unconscious and injured, having defended his sister from Bob Ewell and narrowly escaped with his life.

Jem learns an important lesson through his relationship with Mrs Dubose. In an angry outburst, prompted by Mrs Dubose calling Atticus a 'nigger-lover', he deliberately slices the tops off all the old lady's camellias. Atticus insists on an apology, and when Mrs Dubose demands that Jem read to her regularly, Atticus makes him do it. Eventually, Jem learns that there is more than one side to Mrs Dubose. Although she is dying, she is bravely trying to overcome drug addiction. Atticus treats her with respect and courtesy which, as usual, provides a role model for Jem to copy.

By the beginning of Part Two Jem is 12 and growing away from Scout, who finds him 'difficult to live with, inconsistent, moody'. But Calpurnia tells her that 'He's gonna want to be off to himself a lot now, doin' whatever boys do'.

Jem, the son of a lawyer, understands the finer points of the trial and the workings of the law in a way that Scout does not. From time to time during the five trial chapters (17–21), he explains to Scout what is happening. He is clearly very interested in the case, and his desperation for Atticus to win has as much to do with his regard for justice as his regard for his father.

As Jem grows up, the reader can see, through Scout, that he is becoming ever more like his father. 'Jem's soft brown hair and eyes, his oval face and snug-fitting ears were our mother's, contrasting oddly with Atticus's greying black hair and square-cut features, but they were somehow alike. Mutual defiance had made them alike' (Chapter 15).

Charles Baker ('Dill') Harris

Dill

* stays in Maycomb with his aunt, Miss Rachel Haverford, each summer
* says of his family 'they do get on a lot better without me. I cannot help them any'
* lives in what Scout describes as 'a twilight world' of escapist make-believe
* joins in with the Boo Radley games at the beginning of the novel
* is with Scout and Jem when the Old Sarum lynching party confronts Atticus
* is with Scout and Jem at the trial
* is used by Harper Lee to provide a contrasting, less stable, family background to the Finches

Conclusions

Dill comes from Meridian in Mississippi. His mother is remarried and, ironically, he does not enjoy the family stability and security that Scout and Jem do with their single parent. Dill looks strange: 'He wore blue linen shorts that buttoned to his shirt, his hair was snow white and stuck to his head like duck-fluff.' He is also

L–R: Jem (Philip Alford) and Scout (Mary Badham) regard Dill (John Megna) as a third sibling

unusually small for his age and he is very bookish. Keen reader as Scout is, she acknowledges that Dill reads two books to her one, which is why he is such an imaginative inventor of colourful stories. He weaves fantasies to cover his own unhappiness. To Scout and Jem, Dill becomes almost a third sibling and Scout misses him intensely when he returns home each autumn.

Dill is curious about Boo Radley and is still trying to interest the others in childish, Radley-connected games two or three years after they first started and when Scout and Jem have grown out of them. In that sense, Harper Lee does not develop the character of Dill and does not allow him to grow up and change as Scout and Jem do.

In Chapter 14, Dill turns up unexpectedly in Scout's bedroom having run away from home. 'They just wasn't interested in me,' he says of his parents, to Scout's amazement. Atticus arranges for Dill to stay. This is just before the lynching party incident and the trial. Therefore, Dill is with Scout and Jem when they creep out to the jail at night and then when they disobey the adults and attend the trial. Dill is upset at the trial and cries at the casual thoughtlessness of Mr Gilmer's cross-examination of Tom Robinson. He is therefore presented as a sensitive child.

Arthur ('Boo') Radley

Boo

* says almost nothing
* never leaves the house during daylight
* is the victim of a bullying brother, Nathan
* is presented by Harper Lee as an almost invisible character
* tries to befriend the children in several ways
* saves Jem's, and probably Scout's, life when they are attacked by Bob Ewell

Conclusions

According to local rumour, Boo Radley, now aged about 48, attacked his father with a pair of scissors 15 years earlier. The family did not want him to be committed to an asylum, so they kept him indoors instead. Old Mr Radley is long since dead and the unpleasant, bullying Nathan Radley seems to be in charge of Boo. Both Atticus and Miss Maudie Atkinson hint to the children that they doubt this story is the whole truth. It could well be a case of a gentle, timid, damaged man — possibly depressed and perhaps with learning difficulties — being cruelly victimised by his family.

Whatever the truth, Boo has not been seen for a long time and that is enough to make the children curious. By constantly discussing it, they whip up a part-pleasurable, part-genuine fear of the Radley house and family in general, and Boo in particular. Harper Lee shows a perceptive understanding of the way children's minds work in her presentation of this part of the plot.

Meanwhile, Boo, presumably knowing that the children are making clumsy approaches to him, would like to be friends. It is well recognised that people who are psychologically damaged may relate better to children (or animals) than to adults. Boo leaves the children little presents in the tree on the path outside the Radley house, until Nathan puts a cruel and abrupt stop to this. It is Boo who finds Jem's trousers, attempts to mend them and leaves them on the fence for collection. He also creeps out unseen while Miss Maudie's

Boo Radley (Robert Duvall) is befriended by Scout at the end of the novel

Universal/The Kobal Collection

house is on fire and puts a blanket around Scout's shoulders, although she does not realise this at the time. Harper Lee makes sure that the reader sees 'past' Scout and works out where the blanket has come from.

Boo's most important action in the novel is to hear the children's shouts when they are being attacked by Bob Ewell and to run silently to their rescue. He kills the attacker with a kitchen knife, an action that Heck Tate — and eventually Atticus — sees as morally justified, so they agree to keep the truth to themselves. We last see Boo standing silently in the shadows, first in Jem's bedroom and then on the veranda, before being led gently home by Scout at his request. She never sees him again.

Calpurnia ('Cal')

Calpurnia

- is the black housekeeper to the Finch family and a mother figure to Scout and Jem
- comes to work daily and has a home of her own elsewhere, although neither Scout nor the reader sees it
- is older than Atticus (who is 50) and has a grown-up family including Zeebo, the refuse collector
- is literate
- has two speech styles: one for the black community and an 'educated' one for when she is with white people
- has firm ideas about behaviour and discipline
- is understanding and wise
- takes the children to First Purchase Church
- is presented by Harper Lee as a fully developed black character and an example of a sensible, respectable working black person with thoughts and feelings
- is the black person Scout knows best

Conclusions

Calpurnia has been with the Finch family all her working life, having worked for Atticus's parents and grandparents at Finch's Landing. Atticus trusts and relies on her totally, describing her in Chapter 14 as a 'faithful member of the family'. When Scout, still only six, treats Walter Cunningham discourteously at lunch, it is Calpurnia who tells Scout 'fiercely' that 'Don't matter who they are, anybody sets foot in this house's yo' comp'ny...if you can't act fit to eat at the table you can just set here and eat in the kitchen!' (Chapter 3). Scout answers back and ends up feeling childishly resentful after a 'stinging smack'. When Scout later suggests to Atticus that he lose no time in dismissing Calpurnia, her father's voice in response is 'flinty': 'I've no intention of getting rid of her, now or ever. We couldn't operate a single day without Cal.'

Later in the novel, Aunt Alexandra seems a little jealous of Calpurnia's warm relationship with the children and worries about their 'friendship' with a black person whose church they have attended and whose home they'd like to visit. In Chapter 14 she suggests that, now she has come to live with Atticus, Scout and Jem, they no longer need Calpurnia. Atticus tells her, 'Calpurnia's not leaving this house until she wants to', adding that 'the children love her'.

Harper Lee shows us another side of Calpurnia (who usually spends much of her time producing meals) through the visit to First Purchase Church in Chapter 12. We see her fussing over their clothes as if Scout and Jem were her own children. We, with Scout, observe her among her own community: Lula, who challenges her for bringing 'white chillun' (Jem and Scout) to the black church; Reverend Sykes, who takes the service; and Zeebo, whom Calpurnia has taught to read. All this is part of Scout's education. 'That Calpurnia led a modest double life never dawned on me. The idea that she had a separate existence outside our household was a novel one, to say nothing of her having command of two languages,' she comments.

Harper Lee uses Calpurnia as a link between the white and black communities. For example, in Chapter 12, it is through her that Scout learns more about the difficulties faced by the Robinson family. Atticus asks her, in Chapter 22, to thank the black community for their gifts to him and it is Calpurnia who Atticus asks, in Chapter 24, to accompany him when he goes to tell Helen Robinson that her husband Tom has been shot.

Bob Ewell

Bob Ewell

- falsely accuses Tom Robinson of raping his daughter, Mayella
- certainly beat Mayella and possibly raped her himself
- is a widower like Atticus
- has a large family ranging from the eldest, Mayella, who is 19, to much younger children including Burris
- lives on state benefits
- drinks and is violent
- is lazy ('the only man I ever heard of who was fired from WPA for laziness', Chapter 27)
- continues to harass Helen Robinson after Tom's death
- attacks the children and breaks Jem's arm
- is killed by Boo Radley to save Jem and Scout

Conclusions

Atticus demonstrates in court that the disabled Tom Robinson could not have struck Mayella's right eye. Bob Ewell, her left-handed father, is, however, an obvious culprit (Chapter 17). Questioned by Atticus (Chapter 18), Mayella effectively admits that her father, although 'tollable', is violent when drunk, but she later retracts this: "Except when he's drinking?" asked Atticus so gently that Mayella nodded.'

Key point

Bob Ewell's extreme laziness is shown by his being fired from the WPA (Works Progress Administration). This organisation was set up during the Depression in 1935 to give work to those who were unemployed. It was rare for anyone to be fired from the WPA.

When Tom Robinson describes to the court Mayella's pitiful attempt to seduce him (Chapter 19), he says 'She says she never kissed a grown man before an' she might as well kiss a nigger. She says what her papa do to her don't count.' Given that Bob Ewell is evidently not an affectionate father like Atticus, we can take this as a hint that Ewell may be a sexual abuser.

Atticus (Gregory Peck) confronts Bob Ewell (James M. Anderson)

Although Tom Robinson is found guilty by the jury (Chapter 21), many people in Maycomb know that he is innocent and that Ewell, by implication, is guilty. Ewell is aware of this and he is deeply resentful of Atticus for having exposed him. That is why, as Scout discovers in Chapter 22, Ewell 'stopped Atticus on the post office corner, spat in his face, and told him he'd get him if it took the rest of his life'.

Bob Ewell is an unusual character in *To Kill a Mockingbird* because Harper Lee presents him without any redeeming features. There is nothing positive to say about him. By any standards, he is a bad father — in contrast with Atticus — and he lies, drinks and does no work. He has nothing useful to contribute to society. In fact, like the rabid dog shot by Atticus in Chapter 10, he is dangerous, as the attack on Scout and Jem shows. This is why it is morally right for Ewell to be killed in Chapter 28 and for Boo Radley not to be punished for it.

Tom Robinson

Tom

- is aged 25, married to Helen and a father of three children
- is well respected in his own black community
- has only one functioning arm following a cotton gin accident when he was 12
- is found guilty of attacking and raping Mayella Ewell
- tries to escape while in prison awaiting appeal
- is shot dead by prison guards

Conclusions

Tom Robinson, 'a black-velvet Negro, not shiny, but soft black velvet' (Chapter 19), is presented as a hard-working cotton picker employed by Link Deas. He is a kindly, family man. He makes time to help Mayella after work because he feels sorry for her (Chapter 20). His wife faints with shock when she learns of his death (Chapter 25) and his children are polite and well cared for (Chapter 20). He has much more in common with Atticus than the white Bob Ewell does.

In Chapter 20, Tom speaks politely and respectfully to the court and is reluctant to describe Mayella's lonely sexual approach to him. As Scout comments in Chapter 19, 'It occurred to me that in their own way, Tom Robinson's manners were as good as Atticus's'. In the incident with Mayella, Tom could not win. Had he turned 'ugly' by pushing or striking her, he would have been arrested for assaulting a white woman, so he ran away instead: 'A sure sign of guilt' (Chapter 20).

Tom Robinson, whose tragedy is at the centre of the novel, is presented as an ideal black man and someone against whom the reader can measure other

Atticus (Gregory Peck) defends Tom Robinson (Brock Peters) in court

characters. Harper Lee makes us feel that his trial and death are deeply regrettable, although there is hope for other black people in a similar position in the future because of the sympathy evoked for Tom by Atticus and others. He is, like Boo Radley, a 'mockingbird'. He harms no one and therefore does not deserve to die.

Miss Maudie Atkinson

Miss Maudie

* is a neighbour of the Finches
* is humane, thoughtful and considerate like Atticus
* is liked by Scout and Jem
* talks to the children both about the Radleys and about the Robinson case
* is a keen gardener
* loses her home in a fire but takes it in her stride
* is critical of many of the other women in the town
* is an old friend of Atticus's brother, Uncle Jack

Conclusions

Miss Maudie's family and the Finches have known each other for several generations. It was, for example, Miss Maudie's aunt, 'old Miss Buford', who taught the infant Calpurnia her letters (Chapter 12) 60 years or so before the opening of *To Kill a Mockingbird*. When Uncle Jack comes to stay, he teases Miss Maudie because they have been friends since childhood (Chapter 5).

Miss Maudie will not join in town gossip and is crisply dismissive of Miss Stephanie Crawford's love of it: 'That is three-fourths coloured folks and one-fourth Stephanie Crawford,' she tells Scout about the Boo Radley rumours (Chapter 5). Scout adds 'Miss Maudie's voice was enough to shut anybody up.' She refuses to go to Tom Robinson's trial, saying of people like Stephanie Crawford in her hat and gloves, that ''t's morbid, watching a poor devil on trial for his life. Look at all those folks, it's like a Roman carnival' (Chapter 16).

The children frequently visit Miss Maudie, who gives them cake and fascinates them with the metal bridge on her teeth. She is never afraid to say what she thinks and often gives them advice and information but, like Atticus, she never talks down to them. She tells them, for example, the truth about the Radleys (Chapter 5) and that she thinks Atticus has achieved something important at the trial (Chapter 22). At Aunt Alexandra's missionary meeting (Chapter 24), Miss Maudie stands out as being different from most Maycomb ladies.

Because of her love of plants (inherited from her doctor father, Chapter 5), Miss Maudie's house is destroyed by fire in Chapter 8. Even in the face of this disaster, Miss Maudie remains unruffled and retains her sense of humour.

Harper Lee presents Miss Maudie as a feminine balance for Atticus and another substitute mother for the children, alongside Calpurnia and Aunt Alexandra. Sensible, balanced and sensitive views like Miss Maudie's express hope for the future of Maycomb. Not everyone is blinded by prejudice.

Other characters

Harper Lee mentions a large number of Maycomb people by name in *To Kill a Mockingbird*. They represent black and white, male and female, youth and age, different social classes and professions and a range of points of view. Together, they function like a chorus in a Greek drama or an opera. Sometimes they speak as individuals. Sometimes groups of them — like the Old Sarum lynching party (Chapter 15) or Aunt Alexandra's ladies (Chapter 24) — share an attitude. They include:

* Aunt Alexandra: Atticus's sister, who leaves her ineffectual husband and comes to live with the Finches in Chapter 12. Rather self-opinionated, she thinks Atticus is raising the children too open-mindedly and wants them to be reminded of

the family's position in Maycomb's 'caste system'. Scout is resentful of her interference, but as time goes on Aunt Alexandra mellows. Although she is appalled by the suggestion that Scout and Jem might be social visitors in Calpurnia's home (Chapter 14), she is sorry that Atticus loses the case (Chapter 22), is genuinely upset that Tom is dead (Chapter 24) and horrified when Jem is attacked by Bob Ewell (Chapter 29). Harper Lee uses her to show us that the conflict and tensions in *To Kill a Mockingbird* are not clear-cut. Sometimes Aunt Alexandra is right. She realises, for example, how dangerous Bob Ewell is when Atticus does not. In her way, she has what she regards as the children's best interests at heart, however irritating Scout finds her.

* Heck Tate: the sheriff who asks Atticus to shoot the rabid dog (Chapter 10). He also gives evidence in court and insists at the end of the novel that he and Atticus will keep to themselves the truth about Bob Ewell's death. He is presented as a decent man who respects Atticus.

* Judge Taylor: presides over the Tom Robinson case, having asked Atticus to conduct the defence. Judge Taylor wants the truth told and knows that only Atticus would have the integrity to defend Tom properly. He is straight and fair in court, even though to Scout's eyes he seems not to be paying attention. Bob Ewell clearly resents him and attempts to burgle Judge and Mrs Taylor's home in the autumn after the trial (Chapter 27). Judge Taylor is another example of a moderate man concerned for justice.

* Dolphus Raymond: well known in the town as a fairly prosperous white man who has married a black woman. His 'mixed' children are sent to the North where they will not encounter prejudice. He is reputed to be a drunk and an 'evil man', but Scout and Dill discover outside the court that it is only Coca-Cola that he carries (Chapter 20). He feigns drunkenness to give people something to criticise him for. His function in the novel is to teach Scout and the reader not to accept things at face value.

Text focus

Look carefully at Chapter 19 from 'I know what you mean, boy' to 'all you gotta do is step back inside the courthouse' in Chapter 20. Read it several times.

> Scout has been told that Dolphus Raymond is an 'evil man' because he drinks. This is the first time she has met him face to face, so although she finds him 'fascinating', with his English riding boots and wholesome smell of 'leather, horses, cottonseed', she accepts his invitation to take a drink 'reluctantly'. Mr Raymond offers Scout and Dill a paper sack with straws in it. He knows what the children think and Scout comments that he was 'evidently taking delight in corrupting a child'. Actually, he is enjoying his own joke because, as Dill discovers when he takes a sip, the bag contains nothing but Coca-Cola.

> Harper Lee is revealing more of Dolphus Raymond's character through Scout's surprise and attitude. He says that he knows he will be criticised. 'Some folks don't — like the way I live' he tells the children, referring to his black wife and 'mixed' children whom the children know by sight. Scout describes him ironically as a 'sinful man who had mixed children and didn't care who knew it'. He argues that letting people think he's a drunk gives people a reason to criticise him. Scout finds his reasoning odd and tells him that it is not honest to make 'yourself out badder'n you are already'. She comments with adult hindsight that he was deliberately perpetuating 'fraud against himself'. She fails to understand, as Atticus probably does, that he is deliberately deflecting criticism away from the people who matter to him — his wife and children.

> When Scout asks Mr Raymond why he has let them discover his 'deepest secret', he tells them it is because they are children and will understand, and he half-jokingly swears them to secrecy.

> The portrayal of Dolphus Raymond reminds the reader that all is not as it seems in Maycomb, where false assumptions are constantly made about people. It also reminds us that the town's racism is not total. Mr Raymond is humane and thoughtful, in his eccentric way. His comment about 'the simple hell people give other people' cuts right to the heart of what *To Kill a Mockingbird* is about.

* In what ways is Atticus 'not a run-of-the-mill' man?

* Sum up what Scout learns from this encounter.

* Link Deas: a white cotton farmer with a large number of black employees. Harper Lee uses this character to show that employers can treat black workers decently (as Atticus does with Calpurnia but Mrs Merriweather does not with Sophy, Chapter 24). Link Deas employs Helen Robinson as a house servant after Tom's death and protects her from Bob Ewell's threats.

* Reverend Sykes: the black pastor at First Purchase Church. He makes the children feel welcome during their visit to the church with Calpurnia in Chapter 12. They see him taking the service and coaxing donations out of his congregation for the support of Helen Robinson. At the trial, he escorts the children in and finds seats for them in the black gallery because they are too late to find anywhere else to sit in the crowded courtroom. When the trial is over, he makes his congregation, and the children, stand up in silent respect for Atticus (Chapter 21). Like Tom Robinson, he is an example of a man who is respected and respectable, and who just happens to be black.

* Mrs Henry Lafayette Dubose: a sick neighbour who criticises and goads Scout and Jem relentlessly, especially about Atticus's decision to defend Tom Robinson. After Jem uncharacteristically loses his temper and slices the tops off her camellias in revenge, Atticus makes him apologise (Chapter 11). Mrs Dubose

then demands that Jem comes regularly to read to her, which Atticus insists he must do (and Scout volunteers too). The old lady is bedridden and clearly very ill. The children find her repugnant. She dies shortly afterwards. Atticus then explains that Mrs Dubose died in great pain because at the end of her life she had been determined to overcome her addiction to morphine, a painkiller. 'She was a great lady,' Atticus tells Scout and Jem, 'the bravest person I ever knew.' Like Dolphus Raymond, she teaches the children and the reader not to make assumptions about people.

* Other members of the Maycomb 'chorus' include Mr Underwood, the Cunninghams, Cecil Jacobs, Miss Rachel Haverford, Mr Avery, Miss Caroline Fisher, Chuck Little, Mayella Ewell, Burris Ewell, Helen Robinson and her children, Lula, Zeebo, Nathan Radley, Mr Horace Gilmer, Mrs Grace Merriweather and Mrs Gertrude Farrow.

Review your learning

1 Who says 'If your father's anything, he's civilized in his heart'?
2 Name the character who says 'Will you take me home?'
3 Name three people who torment Scout and Jem about their father's intention to defend a 'nigger'.
4 Why does Scout resent Aunt Alexandra when she first arrives?
5 We never see Tom Robinson at home with his family because Scout never visits there. How does Harper Lee get information about Tom to the reader?
6 What makes Bob Ewell an unusual character in the novel compared with almost everyone else?
7 Whom does Miss Maudie criticise most?
8 How does Harper Lee make her characters interesting?
9 Which character in *To Kill a Mockingbird* is the most fully presented in your view?

Themes

> ➤ What are the novel's main themes?
> ➤ What do they add to the novel?
> ➤ How do themes work?
> ➤ What do you learn about Harper Lee's views from the themes she explores in *To Kill a Mockingbird*?

A theme is an idea, or a set of ideas, that is threaded through a piece of writing. Think of *To Kill a Mockingbird* as a piece of multi-coloured fabric. A theme is a single-coloured thread — red, blue, yellow and so on. Each thread is woven into the whole as part of the pattern. It mixes with the other colours that it crosses to make shapes or new colours. All the threads overlap. In the same way, Harper Lee weaves her ideas about family life, growing up or courage into the story that she is telling.

When we discuss a theme, it is as if we are pulling out a single thread from the novel's overall pattern. We can look at it on its own and then weave it back into the whole.

The themes in *To Kill a Mockingbird* that we will consider here are:

* racism
* family
* mockingbirds
* courage
* growing up
* suffering caused by others

Key point

A theme is an idea or issue that links the details of the novel.

Lesser, but related, themes in the novel include:

* elimination of the dangerous for the benefit of the majority
* education
* hypocrisy
* tolerance
* justice

Remember the following three points as you think about the themes in this novel:

1 No theme in a novel is completely separate from any other. They all overlap as in a piece of woven fabric. That is what makes a text such as *To Kill a Mockingbird* feel complete, well constructed and satisfying.

2 Similar themes are often discussed using different names. For example, prejudice is close to intolerance, bigotry to hypocrisy, learning to education. Do not get too carried away in compiling long, repetitive lists of themes.

3 Some themes feature more regularly than others in the pattern of the novel.

Racism

During the trial (Chapter 20), Dolphus Raymond speaks to Scout, Jem and Dill about 'the simple hell that people give other people — without even thinking'. This phrase sums up much of the thoughtless cruelty Harper Lee criticises through her novel. Most, though not all, of this cruelty is caused by racism. Mr Raymond goes on to say that in a few years Dill will grow out of crying 'about the hell white people give coloured folks, without even stopping to think they're people, too'.

Mr Raymond is a wealthy, white man who, unusually for that time, is married to a black woman. He sends his 'mixed' children North as soon as they are old enough. He wants to protect them from Southern prejudice.

Through the pages of *To Kill a Mockingbird* the reader witnesses the commonplace racism of 1930s Alabama. Harper Lee makes sure we continually hear black people being derided and insulted as 'niggers', and the plot makes it clear that blacks are regarded as sub-human by the white community. For

During the 1930s, racial segregation was evident in all aspects of everyday life

example, one of the reasons why Maycomb's whites so readily accept Tom Robinson's guilt is belief in the commonly held racial stereotype that black men had animalistic sexual urges and little self-control. Tom is seriously disabled, having had an accident in his youth while working on a cotton gin. Therefore, with only one good arm, he would almost certainly have been physically unable to overpower Mayella Ewell. Despite this powerful evidence, Tom is not thought worthy of a fair trial by many Maycomb inhabitants. That is why the lynching party, which includes Mr Cunningham, descends on the jail in Chapter 15. For the Robinson family, this racism is a form of hell, which leads to Tom's death at the hands of the white guards who casually shoot him when he panics and tries to scale the prison fence in a desperate escape attempt.

There are many other instances of racism in the novel. Nathan Radley shoots at an imaginary black man when he thinks he is being burgled. Mrs Merriweather cruelly fails to understand what her servant Sophy is feeling.

The black characters, entirely realistically, are depicted as having low expectations and obtaining only low-paid jobs. This is shown as a direct consequence of their segregated and poor quality education — there are no blacks at Scout and Jem's school. Calpurnia can read and write, but she is unusual. At her church, so few members of the congregation are literate that hymns are sung line by line in response to a leader who reads out the words. Cal has taught her son Zeebo, who leads the hymn-singing, to read using the Bible and one of Atticus's law books. Even so, there are no good jobs for the black community. Zeebo is a refuse collector (it is his job to dispose of the corpse of the rabid dog in Chapter 10) and he thinks he has done well. Although black people are used to this, and are reasonably cheerful about it, it all adds up to a detailed picture of casual cruelty.

Family

In *To Kill a Mockingbird*, Harper Lee presents us with a number of different families, some happier and more successful than others. Some are more prominent and others are mentioned only in passing. Families in the novel include the Finches, Radleys, Ewells, Robinsons, Cunninghams, Dill's family and Calpurnia's family. Harper Lee is inviting us to think about different models of family life, to make comparisons and to draw our own conclusions.

However, because the story is told through Scout's narration, the Finch family is the only one that the reader can 'enter'. All the others are viewed from the outside. We are therefore led to compare other families with the Finches as Harper Lee develops this theme.

Atticus Finch is a widower and a single parent, which could, if he had a different personality, have meant that his children were disadvantaged or emotionally deprived. In fact, because he is an intelligent, loving father, he provides his

The Finch family is very close in the novel

children with everything they need. There is a lot of conversation in the Finch home. Atticus talks to his children, teaches them things and listens to what they say. Notice how often Scout, who's only six when the novel opens, sits on her father's lap or close to him while they are talking. He also reads to her regularly. When Jem is injured at the end of the novel, Atticus will not leave his side.

Harper Lee is presenting us with her ideal father. He can be firm (look at the way he rebukes Scout in Chapter 14, although, as Harper Lee makes clear afterwards, he has some sympathy with her point of view) but the children are secure because they know what the family rules are. Atticus, who is at work during the day and sometimes has to stay away overnight, is assisted in his parenting first by Calpurnia and later in the novel by his sister Alexandra.

Aunt Alexandra is part of the extended Finch family. We also meet her grandson Francis, with whom Scout quarrels (Chapter 9), and her nondescript husband Uncle Jimmy. The third sibling is Uncle Jack, a doctor in the North, who returns to Finch's Landing each year for Christmas. In this way — and also through Calpurnia, who has been with the Finch family all her working life — Harper Lee makes us aware of the stock from which Atticus and his children have developed.

Contrasting with the Finch family are the Ewells and the Radleys. Bob Ewell, like Atticus, is a widower. However, he is so lazy that he is sacked from his WPA post (Chapter 27). Instead of working, he prefers to live on state benefits and to spend most of his money on drink. His large family of children are dirty, unmanageable (see the incident in Chapter 3 concerning Burris Ewell — 'the filthiest human being I had ever seen') and allowed to run wild. Mayella, the eldest, is supposed to care for the others, but she is totally incompetent because nothing in her upbringing has trained her for this role (Chapter 18). Her father is violent towards her and, it is hinted, there may be sexual abuse. This family is as far away from the Finches as it is possible to be, yet they live in the same town.

Another unsatisfactory family to contrast with the Finches are the neighbouring Radleys. Boo is damaged and vulnerable — and is rumoured to have attacked his father years earlier with scissors — but no one in his family seems to treat him with the kindness and understanding he might have received if he had been born a Finch. His father has died and his domineering brother Nathan is in charge. Nathan Radley shoots wildly when he thinks he is being burgled by a black man (Chapter 6). He also stops his brother's habit of trying to make contact with Scout and Jem by leaving gifts in the tree (Chapter 7). When old Mrs Radley dies, the community hardly notices. This is an unhappy family without children: neither brother is married so there is no real family life in the Finch sense.

Pause for thought

Are there any 'bad' or 'wicked' families in *To Kill a Mockingbird*, or are there just some who are more fortunate than others? Note that Atticus Finch is a highly educated man but Bob Ewell is barely literate. To what extent can families control what happens to them? What do you think Harper Lee's view is?

Dill, who spends his summers in Maycomb with his aunt, has a mother, father and stepfather back home in Meridian, Mississippi. He tells Scout in Chapter 14 that no one has any time for him at home. Given her own family experience, Scout simply cannot imagine or understand this: 'I found myself wondering...what I would do if Atticus did not feel the necessity of my presence, help and advice. Why, he couldn't get along a day without me. Even Calpurnia couldn't get along unless I was there. They needed me.'

The brief glimpse Harper Lee gives us of the Robinson family at home (Chapter 25) reminds the reader that family contentment and affection does not depend on being financially well off. Neither does it depend on skin colour. The clean, pig-tailed Robinson toddler smiles happily at Atticus. The Robinson boys are polite and playing sensibly together. Everything is orderly and different from, say, the Ewell household. Another black family of which we get a fleeting picture is Calpurnia's. With limited resources, she has taught her son Zeebo to read. He now has a family of his own and works as a refuse collector, so the children know him and see him leading hymns at the First Purchase Church in Chapter 12.

The Cunninghams are also contrasted with other families. Look at the occasion when Walter comes for lunch in Chapter 3, at the background about

Mr Cunningham in Chapter 2 and at the arrival of the lynching party from Old Sarum in Chapter 15. They are poor but hard-working, sometimes misguided but decent. One of the most powerful moments in the novel comes in Chapter 15 when Scout's innocent intervention suddenly makes Mr Cunningham remember family values.

Mockingbirds

A mockingbird is a member of the finch family. Its feathers are dull grey but it sings distinctively and often imitates (mocks) the calls of other birds. There are various species, all native to North America, although some are now endangered. For more information see www.birdsforever.com/mock.html

In *To Kill a Mockingbird*, the bird symbolises innocence and natural goodness, and Harper Lee gives it thematic status. Like Tom Robinson and Boo Radley, mockingbirds are harmless and therefore should not be shot, killed or persecuted. When Atticus gives the children their airguns in Chapter 10, he says 'Shoot all the bluejays you want, if you can hit 'em, but remember it's a sin to kill a mockingbird'. This is the only time Scout ever hears Atticus use the word 'sin', and he seems very firm, so she takes notice. In fact, this is not an original saying. Harper Lee is making Atticus quote an old proverb that occurs in folk stories and other American writing. For example, a poem published in 1900 by Walt Whitman (1819–92) begins 'Out of the cradle endlessly/ Out of the mockingbird's throat, the musical shuttle.'

Paul J. Fusco/SPL

A mockingbird — a symbol of innocence and natural goodness

Because Scout is puzzled by Atticus's reference to sin, she asks Miss Maudie about it. Miss Maudie says: 'Mockingbirds don't do one thing but make music for us to enjoy. They don't eat up people's gardens, don't nest in corncribs, they don't do one thing but sing their hearts out for us. That's why it's a sin to kill a mockingbird.' As the novel develops, Harper Lee uses the mockingbird as a reminder that it is wrong to hurt defenceless or vulnerable people.

Tom Robinson is like a mockingbird, partly because he is physically disabled. He is also socially 'disabled', his real weakness. He is a black man to whom a white woman has made sexual advances. Therefore, in the eyes of most people in Maycomb, he must be destroyed. Boo Radley's likeness to a mockingbird comes about because he is psychologically damaged. He is timid, childlike and almost incapable of being integrated into Maycomb society. He is an outsider and not properly understood, so he is seen as threatening. In this way, Harper Lee draws the elements of her mockingbird theme together by making us compare different characters and events in the novel.

She reinforces the point in Chapter 25 by making Mr Underwood, the newspaper proprietor and editor, write for his readers after the death of Tom Robinson that it 'was a sin to kill cripples, be they standing, sitting, or escaping'. Scout tells us that Mr Underwood 'likened Tom's death to the senseless slaughter of songbirds by hunters and children'.

In Chapter 28, when the children set off for the pageant, they hear a 'solitary' mocking-bird. When it starts to sing, they are immediately in front of the Radley house and the bird is unaware of 'whose tree he sat in'. This is a clear linking of the mockingbird with Boo Radley, who is not at home. He is outdoors somewhere — fortu-nately for the children, whom he rescues from Bob Ewell's attack later that evening.

> **Pause for thought**
>
> Some commentators on *To Kill a Mockingbird* say that Atticus is another 'mockingbird' because he 'sings his heart out' for Tom Robinson in court. How far do you agree with this?

At the end of the novel, Heck Tate tells Atticus that to bring Boo Radley to 'justice' would be a sin. 'It's a sin and I'm not about to have it on my head,' he says. When Scout explains to Atticus that she understands this, she says 'Well, it'd be sort of like shootin' a mockingbird, wouldn't it?'

Text focus

Look carefully at Chapter 31 from '"Will you take me home?"' to 'Just standing on the Radley porch was enough.' Read it several times.

> This passage relates to the novel's family theme because, as she stands on the Radley family porch, Scout reflects on the previous three years, seeing herself and Jem as 'Boo's children'. She also sees Boo for the first time as someone who belongs to the neighbourhood, which is an extension of the family. By presenting a rapid flashback using the third person ('he', 'they', 'the children', 'a man'), Scout sees events from a viewpoint outside her own and links together everything that has happened and all the themes in the novel, the climax of which is her ability to stand, with tolerance and understanding, in Boo's shoes — or at least on his porch.

> 'Boo's children needed him' is a simple, four-word statement. It is poignant because Boo is a cowed, timid individual, ill-treated by his family and misun-derstood by most Maycomb inhabitants, such as Miss Stephanie Crawford. Note that Miss Stephanie is mentioned three times in this passage because her gossipy

judgemental character represents everything that makes Maycomb a 'tired old town' and contributes to its racism, intolerance and insularity, which are threaded thematically though the novel. Yet, like everyone else, Boo thrives on being needed. He has long observed the children from a distance and wanted to be friends with them. When they are attacked in the wood by Bob Ewell, Boo can, at last, do something positive. He is a gentle, childlike person, which is why Harper Lee makes Scout use words like 'whispered', 'gently' and 'afraid'.

- What is there in this passage to remind you that Boo Radley is a 'mockingbird'?
- What words and phrases show how much Scout has grown up in the three years covered by the novel?
- Who shows courage in this passage? What words and phrases show this?

Courage

It is not difficult to find examples of various sorts of courage in *To Kill a Mockingbird*. Examples include Scout's insistence on going with Jem to Mrs Dubose's house (Chapter 11), Chuck Little's refusal to be intimidated by Burris Ewell (Chapter 3), Helen Robinson's stoicism when she is widowed (Chapter 27), Miss Maudie coping with the loss of her home (Chapter 8), Atticus waiting at the jail for the lynch mob (Chapter 15), Mrs Dubose overcoming her morphine addiction (Chapter 11), the children braving the Radley house (Chapter 4) and timid Boo Radley confronting Bob Ewell (Chapter 28).

Atticus's moral courage is Tom Robinson's only hope during his trial

In the Southern states in the 1930s, there was a long-established general approval of 'shot-gun' courage. An example of this is Nathan Radley shooting at 'niggers' when he thinks he is being burgled (Chapter 6), or the men from Old Sarum who think it is brave and right to go to the jail and demand that Tom Robinson be handed over to them (Chapter 15). It is a fierce, reckless kind of courage and is essential to the character of the Southern 'gentleman'. Atticus, of course, does not have it, which is what Scout means when she comments in Chapter 10: 'Atticus was feeble: he was nearly fifty.' The children wish they could show off about his 'manliness' like their schoolmates, whose fathers do the sorts of jobs that Atticus does not. 'He worked in an office, not in a drug-store. Atticus did not drive a dump-truck for the county, he was not the sheriff, he did not farm, work in a garage, or do anything that could possibly arouse the admiration of anyone,' comments the adult Scout looking back with irony, because, of course, Atticus was doing a great deal that was highly admirable. When Atticus shoots the rabid dog, Jem is delighted because, at last, he has discovered in his father a 'manly' skill that makes him more like other fathers.

Key point

Harper Lee does not particularly admire physical courage. She leads the reader to share her view of the importance of the kind of moral courage shown by Atticus.

Harper Lee wants Scout and Jem — and, through Scout, the reader — to understand that moral courage is far more important, and perhaps harder to achieve, than physical courage. Atticus comments in Chapter 11 that Mrs Dubose was 'the bravest person I ever knew', telling the children, 'I wanted you to see what real courage is, instead of getting the idea that courage is a man with a gun in his hand.' This, coming right at the end of the first half of the novel, prepares the reader for the events of the second half.

Atticus defends Tom Robinson because he believes, with passion and with courage, that he must. The fact that he knows he cannot succeed makes his determination even braver. Atticus's moral courage is Tom's only hope at the trial. However, being true to his beliefs is difficult for Atticus; he is abused by townspeople such as Mrs Dubose (Chapter 11), Cecil Jacobs (Chapter 9) and his great-nephew Francis (Chapter 9). He knows that Scout and Jem have to bear this also. At the end of the novel, they are physically attacked by Bob Ewell because of their father's 'nigger-loving' beliefs and moral courage.

Harper Lee is clearly using this theme to suggest that what 1930s Alabama needed was more men like Atticus, who choose to put down their guns and prejudices and 'fight with their heads'. He is contrasted with Bob Ewell, who takes advantage of his daughter, tries to kill the Finch children and lacks all forms of

courage. Harper Lee is also making a comment about Atticus's qualities as a parent. He is bringing up his children in an enlightened Christian way so that they too develop moral courage. We see this, for example, as Scout gradually learns to cope with the comments about her father without resorting to fist fights.

Growing up

The novel covers a period of three years during which time Harper Lee presents Scout and Jem (and, to a lesser extent, Dill) growing up and changing. This happens partly because time is passing and partly because they are exposed to a series of planned and unplanned 'lessons'. You can take almost any chapter of *To Kill a Mockingbird* and find answers to the question: 'How does Harper Lee develop Scout's awareness and knowledge in this chapter?' As in real life, growing up is a continuous process.

Most of Scout's learning comes from Atticus, who teaches her to control her impulsiveness (Chapter 9) and to recognise different sorts of courage (Chapters 10 and 11). He also tells her several times that tolerance and empathy ('another person's skin') are important and that sometimes you have to rise above other people's comments and attitude: 'You might hear some ugly talk about it at school, but do one thing for me if you will: you just hold your head high and keep those fists down. No matter what anybody says to you, don't you let 'em get your goat' (Chapter 9).

However, Atticus is not Scout's only source of knowledge. She is also taught manners by Calpurnia when Walter Cunningham comes to lunch (Chapter 3) and the value of being a 'lady' by Aunt Alexandra (Chapter 24). Uncle Jack teaches her something about adult perceptions of children (Chapter 9). From the teachers at school (Miss Caroline in Chapters 2 and 3, and Miss Gates in Chapter 26) she learns that many 'educated' adults are much less wise and more prejudiced and ignorant than Atticus.

Ironically, Scout believes she acquires little formal learning at school. She is more advanced than most of the other children and the teachers are not skilled in what would now be called mixed-ability teaching: 'I inched sluggishly along the treadmill of the Maycomb County school system' and 'I knew nothing except what I gathered from *Time* magazine and reading everything I could lay hands on at home' (Chapter 4).

Jem's increasing maturity is carefully charted through the novel too. Scout comments on the changes she notices, especially at the beginning of Part 2 when Jem is 12. She is puzzled by the change in him, which 'had come about in a matter of weeks'. Calpurnia, herself the mother of at least one grown-up son, Zeebo, understands and tells Scout that Jem is 'gonna want to be off by himself a lot now, doin' whatever boys do'.

The growing separation of brother and sister had begun earlier, however. Scout tells us in Chapter 6, when Jem goes to get his trousers, that 'Jem and I began to part company'. During the compelled visits to Mrs Dubose (Chapter 11) Scout notices her brother acquiring 'an alien set of values'. Later, in Chapter 12, Jem advises Scout to be more respectful of their aunt by 'bein' a girl and acting right'. In Chapter 14, he breaks 'the remaining code of our childhood' by going to tell Atticus about Dill's secret arrival in the Finch house. It is also at about this time that Calpurnia starts to treat Jem as an adult by addressing him as 'Mister Jem'. Jem has come a long way since the childish Boo Radley games in the first few chapters of the novel.

During the trial, it is the maturing Jem who explains to Scout what is going on and why, although he is deeply distressed by the outcome (Chapter 22). His face 'streaked with angry tears', he is having difficulty coming to terms with the reality of the adult world facing him.

Harper Lee emphasises the obvious point that all children learn from those around them. As Scout and Jem are Atticus's children, whom he respects and nurtures, they are on their way to becoming caring, sensitive adults. However, had they been born into another family, such as the Ewells or the Cunninghams, they could just as easily have grown up to be unjust, prejudiced and selfish, victims of 'Maycomb's usual disease'.

Understanding themes

A good way to develop your understanding of the themes in any literary text is to create a spider diagram, similar to the example below, for each one. Write the title of the theme you want to investigate in a box in the middle of a clean sheet of paper. Around the outside, write notes on events in the text that relate to that theme. You may find it helpful to construct a spider diagram for each main theme as a revision exercise.

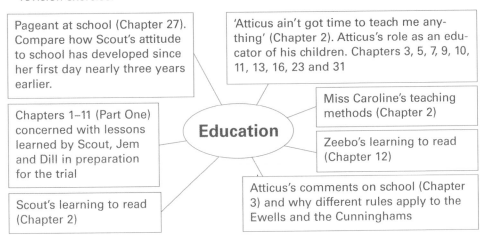

Pageant at school (Chapter 27). Compare how Scout's attitude to school has developed since her first day nearly three years earlier.

'Atticus ain't got time to teach me anything' (Chapter 2). Atticus's role as an educator of his children. Chapters 3, 5, 7, 9, 10, 11, 13, 16, 23 and 31

Chapters 1–11 (Part One) concerned with lessons learned by Scout, Jem and Dill in preparation for the trial

Education

Miss Caroline's teaching methods (Chapter 2)

Zeebo's learning to read (Chapter 12)

Scout's learning to read (Chapter 2)

Atticus's comments on school (Chapter 3) and why different rules apply to the Ewells and the Cunninghams

Suffering caused by others

The 'simple hell' people impose on each other in *To Kill a Mockingbird* goes beyond the treatment of black people by whites. Consider the plight of Mayella Ewell. She lives with a brutal and drunken father who may be forcing her to have an incestuous sexual relationship with him. She has no money and no friends. Young as she is, she is expected to look after all the younger children. Part of Tom Robinson's 'crime' is that he, a happily married and decent family man, feels sorry for her — not something the prejudiced community approves of in a black man.

Dill is a deeply unhappy boy too. For all his fantasising ('no one could tell them like Dill could') he is an unwanted child whose mother, far away in Mississippi, is too busy with her new husband to take any notice of him. Boo Radley suffers as well. He is a damaged and vulnerable human being, tyrannised first by his father and now by his brother.

Key point

'Man's inhumanity to man/ Makes countless thousands mourn!' is a phrase from the poem 'Man Was Made To Mourn' by the Scottish poet, Robert Burns (1759–96). So many characters in *To Kill a Mockingbird* are guilty of causing suffering that it could be viewed as a theme in its own right. Think about Nathan Radley, Bob Ewell, Aunt Alexandra, Stephanie Crawford, Mrs Dubose, Scout when Walter Cunningham comes to lunch, the three children trying to entice Boo, and many other examples.

Review your learning

1 What do we mean by a theme?
2 List the most important themes in *To Kill a Mockingbird*.
3 Who are the main 'mockingbirds' in the novel?
4 What is the main sort of courage that interests Harper Lee?
5 What did Dolphus Raymond mean by 'the simple hell that people give other people'?
6 Which character in *To Kill a Mockingbird* do you think grows up and changes the most?

Style

> How does the author tell her story?
> From whose points of view does the reader learn about events and characters?
> Where and when is the novel set and what effect does this have?
> How does Harper Lee create atmosphere?
> What use does she make of colourful description?
> What sort of language does she use and why?

Viewpoint

The story is told entirely by Jean Louise ('Scout') Finch. As she is part of the events she is describing, Scout the narrator uses pronouns such as 'I', 'me', 'mine', 'we', 'us' and 'ours'. This technique is known as a **first-person narrative**. Many famous books have been written in this format, including *Oliver Twist* by Charles Dickens (1838), *Jane Eyre* by Charlotte Brontë (1848), *The Illustrated Mum* by Jacqueline Wilson (2000) and *The Curious Incident of the Dog in the Night-Time* by Mark Haddon (2003).

Although first-person narratives are realistic, writing in this style presents the author with technical problems which would not exist if the story were told in the third person, i.e. by someone outside the story describing the activities, thoughts and views of the characters. **Third-person narratives** use pronouns such as 'he', 'she', 'his', 'her', 'they', 'their' and 'theirs'. J. K. Rowling's Harry Potter books and Michelle Magorian's *Goodnight Mr Tom* (1981) are examples of third-person narratives.

In a first-person narrative such as *To Kill a Mockingbird*, the story is restricted to events witnessed by the narrator. Harper Lee gets around this fairly easily and smoothly by using other characters to give Scout information. When Scout tells the story of Simon Finch in Chapter 1, she is relying on what other people have told her. Most of her background information about the Radleys comes from Miss Maudie and Atticus as they try to make the children see that they must not believe town gossip. Dill tells Scout about the visit to the Robinson house in Chapter 25. Sometimes Scout overhears things, such as the conversation between Atticus and Uncle Jack in Chapter 9 and between Atticus and Aunt Alexandra in Chapter 14.

Harper Lee does not restrict herself to one point of view. Other opinions are simply filtered through Scout, and the reader learns to allow for a child's exaggerations and distortions. When Atticus is telling Scout why she has to go to school in Chapter 3 although the Ewells do not, we can see 'past' Scout and understand Atticus's point of view. Similarly, when Aunt Alexandra expresses concern about Scout's lack of family awareness and femininity (Chapter 23), we share Scout's frustration but at the same time Harper Lee also makes sure we understand Aunt Alexandra's point of view. Another example is Lula's racist confrontation of the white children at First Purchase Church in Chapter 12. We share Scout and Jem 's uncomfortable feelings, but we can understand why Lula feels as she does.

Remember that there are two Scouts in *To Kill a Mockingbird*. There is the young girl aged six to nine who lives in the early 1930s, and there is the adult Scout looking back many years later describing her memories: 'When enough years had gone by to enable us to look back on them, we sometimes discussed the events leading to his [Jem's] accident,' she says in the second paragraph of the novel.

Although the child Scout is the main character in the story, it is the adult Scout who is the narrator. Although we never 'meet' the adult Scout and know nothing directly about her after the age of nine, Harper Lee's use of this 'hidden' adult narrator enables her to use adult language and to express things from an adult point of view.

The young Scout would never have said 'After one altercation' (Chapter 12), 'No economic fluctuations changed their status' (Chapter 17) or 'and our classmates mercifully let us forget our father's eccentricities' (Chapter 27). Harper Lee is making her narrator look back and interpret in adult language what she felt and did as a child.

Text focus

Look carefully at the opening of Chapter 16, from the start to 'She knows what she means to this family'. Read it several times.

> Jem and Scout (with Dill) have disobediently left the house the previous evening and gone to the town jail where Atticus was protecting Tom Robinson with his presence. Aunt Alexandra radiates 'waves of disapproval' as she sips her breakfast coffee. She is cold in her manner and cross because 'children who slipped out at night were a disgrace to the family'. Calpurnia, on the other hand, is presented here as much warmer and more loving. She gives into Scout's pleading, as a gesture of sympathy, and gives her a drop of coffee with plenty of comforting milk while Aunt Alexandra issues a 'warning frown'. She is put out because Atticus has been humorously commenting on Braxton Underwood's self-contradictory attitude to blacks, which Aunt Alexandra thinks is inappropriate in front of Calpurnia. The point here is that Atticus and the children regard Calpurnia as a member of the family. To Aunt Alexandra, she

is just a servant, one of 'them', before whom certain things should not be said. Perhaps, too, Aunt Alexandra is jealous of Calpurnia's status in the family. The children's aunt has moved in to be a substitute mother, but Calpurnia is already warmly fulfilling that role. These subtleties are embedded in the style.

➢ Scout is looking back and analysing what happened and what people felt from an adult perspective. As a child, she would not have used expressions like 'frank admiration', 'fey fit of humour' or 'outright irritation', yet her childishness is clearly presented through the use of expressions she would have used at the time such as 'awfully nice'.

➢ Jem is presented here as having been distressed the previous evening but feeling stronger this morning. That's why he can eat three eggs for breakfast. Atticus is not angry with his children for following him into town the night before. He teases his sister and annoys her: 'Atticus said he was right glad his disgraces had come along.' His mood turns though when Aunt Alexandra criticises his attitude to Calpurnia and a 'faint starchiness' comes into his voice as he declares that 'Anything fit to say at the table's fit to say in front of Calpurnia'.

✳ What do you learn here — through Scout from Atticus — about Braxton Underwood?

✳ Look at the balance Harper Lee uses in this passage between **direct speech** ('he asked') and **reported speech** ('children who slipped'). How well do you think this mixture works? Explain your views.

Setting and atmosphere

The novel is set almost entirely in Maycomb, an imaginary town in Alabama based on Monroeville, Harper Lee's home town (see page 6). Only once, and very briefly, does the action shift anywhere else — when Atticus takes the children a few miles out of town to spend Christmas with his sister's family at Finch's Landing (Chapter 9).

Other places are mentioned. Dill arrives each summer from Meridian in the neighbouring state of Mississippi, Atticus is often away working in Alabama's state capital Montgomery, Uncle Jack visits from the North and Tom Robinson is imprisoned and dies at a jail some distance from Maycomb. However, Scout and Jem stay in Maycomb — 'a tired old town'.

Many of the town's inhabitants have limited vision because they have no experience of any other location and therefore find it difficult to see things in a wider perspective. They are 'narrow minded' partly because of where and how they live. Harper Lee makes fun of this insularity when she presents us with the Maycomb Missionary Society ladies in Chapter 24. They think they care deeply

about an impoverished tribe in remote Africa, but are hard and unfeeling about poor black residents in their own community.

The Maycomb setting is crucial to what happens in *To Kill a Mockingbird*. Tom Robinson's conviction would not have happened in the Northern states of America (where Dolphus Raymond sends his children to protect them from prejudice, and where Uncle Jack practises as a doctor). In the North, slavery was never part of everyday life and so large communities of poor, disadvantaged blacks did not develop as they did in the South after slaves were freed.

Remember that the novel is set in a particular time, as well as a particular location. The early 1930s was a time of great poverty for Southern farmers and their surrounding communities following the Wall Street Crash of 1929 (see page 9). Partly because of the poverty, and partly because slavery had still existed in relatively recent times, there was tension between the different racial groups in the Southern states in the 1930s. It is this atmosphere that Harper Lee depicts so effectively in *To Kill a Mockingbird*. As you study the novel, pay attention to the way in which Lee uses literary style to reflect the tension in events.

As soon as word gets out that Atticus will defend Tom Robinson, the comments start: 'we would squirm our way through sweating sidewalk crowds and sometimes hear "There's his chillun"' or "Yonder's some Finches"' (Chapter 14). Although the young Scout does not understand the implications of some of this and, on one occasion, goes home to ask Atticus what rape is, she is well aware that animosity is building up. The tension is tightened through the aggressive remarks of Francis Finch, Cecil Jacobs and most particularly the 'vicious' Mrs Dubose (Chapter 11). Because Mrs Dubose is an adult, it hurts more, and her comments inflame Jem so that he loses his temper and vandalises her garden.

The atmosphere in court is dramatic and tense because a number of people are 'performing' in public, including Atticus, Judge Taylor and all the people who give evidence. Yet no one can be sure of the outcome. Atticus tells Scout in Chapter 9 that there is no chance of his winning the case for Tom. Reverend Sykes tells the children, 'I ain't ever seen any jury decide in favour of a coloured man over a white man' (Chapter 21).

Harper Lee builds up suspense by running the trial through several chapters and taking the children out for breaks. There is a great sense of disappointment when the jury returns its guilty verdict in Chapter 21. Jem weeps bitterly at the beginning of Chapter 22. Atticus shows signs of strain, too, for the first time: 'Seems that only children weep,' he comments bitterly in Chapter 22. He is clearly exhausted, although brighter the following morning.

The last third of the book takes place after the trial and Harper Lee builds up an atmosphere of suspense in anticipation of Bob Ewell's attack. She does this by having Scout mention seemingly trivial things like Ewell spitting at Atticus, losing his job and being suspected of an attempted break-in at Judge Taylor's house.

Atticus sees no threat but Aunt Alexandra is convinced (rightly, as it turns out) that Ewell will attempt something 'furtive'. As the children leave for the pageant, Scout solemnly mentions setting out on 'our longest journey together', which signals to the reader that something dramatic is coming (Chapter 27).

In the wood, on their return journey, a tense atmosphere of fear and danger is created and heightened by Scout's being encased in her pageant costume. She cannot see what is going on. The reader can only experience what she can remember feeling, hearing and smelling: 'the soft swish of cotton', 'I felt the sand go cold under my feet', 'His stomach was soft but his arms were like steel'.

The novel ends in an atmosphere of great peace and tranquillity. Jem is asleep, Bob Ewell is dead, Atticus is overwhelmed with relief, Aunt Alexandra is so overcome with (unfounded) guilt that she withdraws from the scene. Scout accompanies the pale, timid Boo Radley home in the moonlight. Atmospherically, this is a scene sharply contrasted with the skirmish in the wood with Ewell and the unjust hostility of the trial. Finally, Scout falls asleep in her own bed.

> **Pause for thought**
>
> Is the ending of *To Kill a Mockingbird* too idealistic and too much like a fairy story? If so, does it spoil your enjoyment of the novel?

Imagery

Imagery means describing one thing by comparing it with pictures of other things.

When Scout refers to Atticus in court, saying 'he'd gone frog-sticking without a light' (Chapter 17), she is using a **metaphor**. She means that Atticus reminds her of someone tackling a task without the proper equipment and she conveys it by making a little picture. When she mentions 'the soft bovine sounds of the ladies' in Chapter 24, she means they sound like cows grazing — and we can imagine that. A metaphor makes the comparison by pretending that the thing or action being described actually *is* the image created.

In Chapter 12, Zeebo's voice is 'like the rumble of distant artillery' and Judge Taylor in Chapter 16 is 'like a sleepy old shark' (seemingly harmless but in reality still ready to bite). These are examples of **similes** — comparisons that use 'as' or 'like' to make it clear that two things are being likened to each other.

Scout also describes things using **personification** — describing the properties of something inanimate (without life) by pretending it has human qualities. In Chapter 1, she mentions the fence as 'a picket drunkenly guarded the front yard' and the house as 'droopy and sick'.

Metaphor, simile and personification are all parts of imagery. Imagery is sometimes called 'figurative language'.

In *To Kill a Mockingbird*, the imagery is carefully drawn from the experience of children growing up in the Southern states, or from books because Scout is a

compulsive reader. Harper Lee makes Scout use colourful and original images based on what would have been the experience of such a child at that place and time. 'Frog-sticking' (stabbing frogs at night that are attracted to a light in the warm, humid climate) is not likely to be a familiar game to a child in Britain today.

Pause for thought

What would be regarded as casual cruelty to animals in Britain today would have been a normal part of life in 1930s Alabama. Harper Lee is not at all judgemental about such issues because attitudes have changed. Find other examples of animal cruelty in *To Kill a Mockingbird*. Then look carefully at the opening of Chapter 25, where a different trend is beginning to develop.

Harper Lee uses imagery to establish character. In Chapter 1, Scout tells us that Calpurnia's 'hand was as wide as a bed slat and twice as hard'. Mayella Ewell's nervousness is stressed by Scout's description of her as 'a steady-eyed cat with a twitchy tail' (Chapter 18). Scout's repugnance at Mrs Dubose is revealed in the imagery she uses: 'Her face was the colour of a dirty pillowcase, and the corners of her mouth glistened with wet, which inched like a glacier down the deep grooves enclosing her chin' (Chapter 11).

Sometimes, Lee uses imagery to evoke a sense of place. The Ewell's home at the rubbish dump, which is very different from Scout's orderly house, is like 'the playhouse of an insane child' (Chapter 17).

Imagery is often linked to **symbolism**. For example, the mockingbird of the title is a metaphor for innocence and vulnerability, which is sustained throughout the novel (see page 62). It takes on the force of a symbol because it is woven into the whole text as a theme rather than being mentioned once for descriptive purposes. Another example of this is Atticus's maxim. He uses the image of getting inside another person's skin and walking around in it as a metaphor for tolerance and understanding. This is more than a description. It is central to the novel.

Language

Harper Lee uses a wide range of language styles for different purposes in *To Kill a Mockingbird*. This is one of the many things that makes it such an interesting and satisfying novel.

Every character, even Atticus, speaks with a broad-vowelled, slow, Southern American accent — different from the more clipped accent of, say, New York. However, on the whole, the more educated the character, the less dialect he or she uses.

Atticus uses mostly standard English and an educated level of vocabulary, even when he is speaking to his children: 'It's slipped into usage with some people like ourselves, when they want a common, ugly term to label somebody,' he tells Scout of the term 'nigger-lover' in Chapter 11. When Dill turns up unexpectedly in Chapter 14, Atticus tells him, 'And for goodness' sake put some of the county back where it belongs, the soil erosion's bad enough as it is.' Dill does not understand. It is Scout, used to her father's sense of humour, who explains, 'He's tryin' to be funny. He means take a bath.'

The children's language is more colloquial than their father's and they speak less precisely with far more **elision** (leaving out letters or syllables). For example, at the end of the novel (Chapter 31), Scout sleepily tells Atticus, 'An' they chased him 'n' never could catch him 'cause they didn't know what he looked like, an' Atticus…' It is Harper Lee's way of reminding us that this is the voice of a child.

At the same time, the children are constantly learning adult vocabulary — especially legal vocabulary — from Atticus. That is why Jem half knows what an entailment is (Chapter 2) and the adult Scout can humorously refer to the runaway Dill as 'the defendant' (Chapter 15). By the end of the novel, Jem's language is more adult than Scout's, which is another reminder that he is four years older and growing up fast.

Less educated characters, both black and white, use more dialect in their speech — words, forms of words and grammar that are not generally used in standard English such as 'chillun' for children and 'suh' for sir. A good example of dialect is Mayella Ewell saying in court (Chapter 18): 'I don't hafta take his sass, I ain't called upon to take it' — which roughly 'translated' into standard English means 'I am not obliged to put up with him [Atticus] making jokes at my expense'. Of course, in context, her meaning is absolutely clear and needs no translation. The same applies to Tom Robinson's reply to Mr Gilmer in court: 'No suh, I didn't go to be' (Chapter 19).

Harper Lee uses language as a way of defining character and creating drama. In court, Bob Ewell declares coarsely that 'I seen that black nigger yonder ruttin' on my Mayella!' (Chapter 17). This crude statement causes such shocked excitement that it takes Judge Taylor five minutes to restore order. He then instructs the witness: 'Mr Ewell, you will keep your testimony within the confines of Christian English usage, if that is possible.' Ewell's aggression in court helps to show the reader what sort of a man he really is. It prepares us for his later attack on the children.

Calpurnia's language links the educated groups in the novel with the uneducated groups. She is one of only four people at her church who can read, although, as Scout wryly observes (Chapter 3), 'when she was furious Calpurnia's grammar became erratic'. When the children go with her to First Purchase Church (Chapter 12), Scout is surprised to discover that Calpurnia has two ways of speaking. She adjusts to the group she is with. 'Now what if I talked white-folks' talk at church, and with my neighbours?' she tells Scout. 'They'd think I was puttin' on airs to beat Moses.' She adds, 'when they don't want to learn there's nothing you can do but keep your mouth shut or talk their language'. Calpurnia is thus presented as being wise, tolerant and adaptable, unlike many Maycomb people.

There are jokes with language in the novel to show that characters are failing fully to understand. Scout uses the word 'morphodite' in Chapter 8 for example. She means 'hermaphrodite' — a creature like her snowman with both male and female characteristics. Bob Ewell does not know the meaning of 'ambidextrous' — able to use right and left hand equally well — and therefore contradicts himself in court (Chapter 17).

The word 'nigger' occurs frequently in *To Kill a Mockingbird*. It comes from the Latin word *niger*, meaning 'black'. The River Niger and the country Nigeria in Africa, where millions of black slaves were captured and taken to America and the Caribbean in the eighteenth and nineteenth centuries, were so named for their 'blackness' by white settlers. Gradually, 'nigger' has become a term of offensive racist abuse, so much so that during the 1995–96 O. J. Simpson murder trial in California the judge would not allow witnesses to use it. They had to say 'the n-word'. It was a little more acceptable in the 1930s than it is now, although Atticus tells Scout not to use it because it is 'common'. Notice that the black people in the novel use it of themselves too. At First Purchase Church, Calpurnia addresses Lula as 'nigger'. Harper Lee, writing in the late 1950s, never uses it directly. She says 'coloured'. You will undoubtedly need to use the word 'nigger' or 'nigger-lover' in your essays. Put inverted commas around these terms to show you are quoting other people's words.

Review your learning

1 What basic story-telling method does Harper Lee use in *To Kill a Mockingbird*?
2 What are the limitations of this method and how does she get around them?
3 What does the novel gain from its setting?
4 For what purposes does Harper Lee use imagery? List as many different uses as you can, giving examples.
5 Why does Harper Lee make Mr Cunningham speak differently from Uncle Jack? List some examples.
6 In view of what you have learned about Harper Lee's style in this section, look closely at this short extract from Chapter 15. Work out in detail the effect of her style in this passage. Jitney Jungle is a supermarket chain — one of the first in America.

> 'Come on,' whispered Jem. We sneaked across the square, across the street, until we were in the shelter of the Jitney Jungle door. Jem peeked up the sidewalk. 'We can get closer,' he said. We ran to Tyndal's Hardware door — near enough, at the same time discreet.
>
> In ones and twos, men got out of the cars. Shadows became substance as light revealed solid shapes moving towards the jail door. Atticus remained where he was. The men hid him from view.
>
> 'He in there, Mr Finch?' a man said.

Tackling the exam

> What sort of questions will you have to answer in the exam?
> How can you plan your answers?
> What is the best way to start and finish essays?
> How should you use quotes?
> What do you have to do to get an A*?

Higher and foundation tier

Higher-tier candidates are provided with a question (or task) and expected to work out for themselves how to structure an answer. If you are entered for the higher tier, you will be asked questions like these in the exam:

1 Atticus told Scout, 'You never really know a man until you stand in his shoes and walk around in them.' What has Scout learned about life from other people's perspectives by the end of the novel?
2 Explain why you think Harper Lee called her novel *To Kill a Mockingbird.*
3 The novel is narrated by a child. What are the advantages and disadvantages of this way of telling a story?
4 How do the characters of Jem and Scout change and mature during the novel?
5 How is the theme of racial prejudice presented in *To Kill a Mockingbird*?
6 Examine the ways in which Harper Lee presents the black community.

Foundation-tier candidates will be asked questions like these. The bullet points below each question suggest an outline framework for the answer:

1 Is Mayella Ewell a victim to feel sorry for or someone to despise because she accuses an innocent man? In your answer comment on:
   * what Mayella says in court
   * what Tom Robinson and Bob Ewell say in court, prompted by Atticus
   * what others say about the Ewell family elsewhere in the novel

2 **How far do you agree that Atticus is an ideal father and citizen? Your answer should consider:**
   * **Atticus's reaction to Scout, Jem and Dill playing games about Boo Radley at the beginning of the novel**
   * **the mad dog episode**
   * **occasions when Atticus talks to his children**
   * **his treatment of Mrs Dubose**
   * **his behaviour at the trial of Tom Robinson**
   * **his attitude to Bob Ewell's threatening behaviour after the trial**
3 **What different sorts of courage are shown in *To Kill a Mockingbird*? Include in your answer what you think about:**
   * **the children's approaches to Boo Radley and his reactions**
   * **the shooting of the mad dog**
   * **Mrs Dubose giving up morphine**
   * **Atticus standing up for justice**
   * **Mr Cunningham turning away from the jail**
   * **Boo Radley killing Bob Ewell**

Pause for thought

As a revision exercise, go through the six higher-tier questions on page 77 and suggest the bullet-point guidance you would expect to see if they were offered at the foundation tier. This is a useful activity whichever tier you are entered for.

As you can see, higher-tier and foundation-tier questions are similar. The main difference is that foundation-tier candidates will receive guidance about how to tackle the question.

Answering the questions

Remember:
* English literature does not have right and wrong answers.
* No two answers, even if they score the same marks, will contain exactly the same material.
* You can answer a question in more than one way and still score high marks.
* All your points must be supported by evidence (quotations or reference to events) from the novel.
* You must do more than retell the story: your job is to demonstrate your knowledge and understanding by commenting on the novel.
* The examiner is interested in your response to *To Kill a Mockingbird* and what you think about it.

There are three main sorts of question — plot, character and theme focused — which you are likely to be asked at GCSE. Here are some examples:

Atticus told Scout, 'You never really know a man until you stand in his shoes and walk around in them.' What has Scout learned about life from other people's perspectives by the end of the novel?

This is a question focusing on the plot — what happens in the novel and how Harper Lee makes it interesting.

How do the characters of Jem and Scout change and mature during the novel?

This question asks you to think about characters and how Harper Lee presents them.

How is the theme of racial prejudice presented in *To Kill a Mockingbird*?

This question asks you to unravel and analyse a major Harper Lee theme.

Planning your answers

Always work out what the question is asking you to do and make a plan before you begin. In an exam, when you are under time pressure, you will have to do this quickly. First, use a highlighter to emphasise the key words in the question, or you could underline them.

Then devise an essay plan — even two or three minutes spent making a plan will pay off. Your answer will be better thought out, better shaped and you are less likely to miss out important points if you have noted them in your plan. This could make the difference between getting a C or D grade and a B, A or A*.

Experiment with different sorts of plan and decide what works for you. Some people like diagrammatic plans. This usually means putting the key idea in a circle in the middle of the page and adding points for inclusion, linked to the key idea, around the outside. Alternatively, make a list and number the points. Below is a plan for the following question.

Atticus told Scout, 'You never really know a man until you stand in his shoes and walk around in them.' What has Scout learned about life from other people's perspectives by the end of the novel?

1 Introduction: Atticus makes this comment about Boo. It also applies to Bob E, Mrs D, Aunt A.

2 Boo — Scout's main lesson from tormenting in Ch 1 to complete understanding at end. Radley porch = symbol.

3 Bob E vicious and lazy — Scout knows no one else like this. Understands eventually he's better dead. Sympathy for Mayella through trial.

4 Mrs D seems spiteful until Scout learns otherwise.

5 Aunt A friction with Scout at first. S gradually develops respect for her point of view — she's right about Bob E.

6 Conclusion: novel could be subtitled 'What Scout Learns'. HL details S's mental development age 6–9 and uses incidents to shape it.

Always 'frame' your answer with an introduction and a conclusion. You are unlikely to be able to make more than four main points in the body of your answer in the time available to you in the exam.

Try to plan your time carefully so that you always complete your answer. However, if you misjudge the time and do not finish, hand in your plan so that the examiner can see where your answer was going.

The sample plan above is, of course, not the only way that this question could be answered. As a revision exercise, devise a plan of your own for a different answer to this question. You might include, for example, what Scout learns about the black community through visiting Calpurnia's church and from hearing Dill's account of Atticus's call on Mrs Robinson to tell her that Tom is dead. Another possibility would be to exclude Mrs Dubose and to bring in a discussion of what Scout learns from, and through, Miss Maudie Atkinson, Nathan Radley, Mr Cunningham and/or Dolphus Raymond.

Essay openings

You will get no marks for copying the question in your opening sentence or paragraph. Instead, your introduction might:

* say how you are going to tackle the question
* interpret the question — say what you think it means
* comment on something that is in the question
* make some general introductory remarks

The examiner's aim is to seek out mark-scoring parts of your essay. You will score marks for making informed analytical comments. Do not waste your limited time writing anything else.

Below are four possible introductions for an essay answering the following question.

How do the characters of Jem and Scout change and mature during the novel?

Introduction 1

Both Scout and Jem change considerably during the course of the novel as they work their way through various incidents and experiences. In this essay, I shall focus on three major factors: their developing understanding of Boo Radley, what they learn about human nature through the trial of Tom Robinson and the influence Atticus has on them.

Introduction 2

This question suggests that Harper Lee has built into the novel a developmental path for Scout and Jem. I agree that she has shown the children growing up and the changes that it brings, although I believe that she presents it more strongly for Jem than for Scout, as I shall show.

Introduction 3

The key word in this question is 'change'. One of Harper Lee's great achievements in *To Kill a Mockingbird* is not only to get right into Scout's mind so that the reader always understands how it feels to be frightened of Boo Radley, admiring of Miss Maudie and so on, but to take us on a journey through growing up. The six-year-old Scout we meet at the beginning of the novel is very different from the maturing nine-year-old we leave on the last page. Through Scout's viewpoint, Harper Lee shows us Jem's shift into adolescence too.

Introduction 4

Scout starts the novel as a child of six who is led by her elder brother and their friend Dill into a childishly irrational fear of Boo Radley. Three years later, when the novel ends, she has spoken to Boo, stood on his porch (in his 'shoes') and recognised the moving truth about him. Jem, meanwhile, has progressed from a less-than-thoughtful ten-year-old to a perceptive young man of 13, acutely interested in law and justice. Harper Lee has brought about these changes by taking the children through a series of experiences.

Essay endings

You will get no extra marks for repeating in your conclusion something that you have said already. In your conclusion, you might:

* summarise your arguments and draw them together in a new way
* make a new point, which you have deliberately held back for the ending

* try to be 'punchy' so that there is a sense of an essay that has been finished rather than just tailing off

Below are three possible conclusions for an essay answering the following question.

How do the characters of Jem and Scout change and mature during the novel?

Conclusion 1

Harper Lee has shown us Scout and Jem being curious about Boo, learning the deceptive truth about Mrs Dubose, and seeing, at first hand during the trial of Tom Robinson, that justice is not fairly applied in 1930s Alabama. Because the author presents them in a range of situations and lets us see and hear them in conversation with wise people like Atticus, Miss Maudie and Dolphus Raymond, we appreciate that, as they change and mature, these children are the hope for Maycomb's future.

Conclusion 2

Scout, who ends the novel thinking back to the child who once stopped at an oak tree 'delighted, puzzled, apprehensive', feels 'very old' and assumes that there is not much more for her and Jem to learn 'except possibly algebra'. Of course she is wrong, and the adult Scout, decades later, is smiling at her younger self. Nonetheless, three years is a long time in the life of a child and Harper Lee has shown us how both children have been changed by, for example, watching the trial, learning to live with their aunt and experiencing the horror of being attacked.

Conclusion 3

To Kill a Mockingbird ends where it began. Jem's arm is 'badly broken at the elbow' and the children have reached a temporary stopping place on a three-year learning curve. Both now know much more about human nature than they did three years earlier, thanks to Tom Robinson, Bob Ewell and Boo Radley, among others.

Using evidence in essays

Just as scientists provide evidence to back up their theories, you need to provide evidence to back up the points in your essay. All the evidence you require lies within the covers of *To Kill a Mockingbird*.

There are two types of evidence:

* Quotation of exact words written in the novel. Look for short phrases that illustrate your point and weave them into your sentences. Always remember to

include quotation marks. You should not need to quote more than one sentence at a time. Aim to work at least eight direct quotations into an exam essay. Structure your sentences like these examples:

Once Jem is 12, Scout finds him 'inconsistent' and 'moody', but Calpurnia, ever perceptive, tells her not to 'fret too much' because the maturing Jem will need to be 'off to himself' and 'doin' whatever boys do'.

As Harper Lee builds up the tension, Scout suddenly realises that their 'company' in the wood has 'shuffled and dragged his feet' before she hears him 'running towards us with no child's steps'.

* Reference to incidents in the novel without quoting directly. You might mention, for example, Lula's attitude to Scout and Jem at First Purchase Church (Chapter 12) as an example of reverse racism without quoting the exact words said. Alternatively, you could mention Heck Tate's deference to Atticus as the better shot when the rabid dog needs killing quickly and efficiently in Chapter 10 as an example of the respect Atticus commands in the community.

Essay writing: ten don'ts

* Don't retell the story.
* Don't make vague statements for which you have no evidence.
* Don't waste your time writing out long quotations that are not grafted tightly into your arguments.
* Don't begin sentences or paragraphs with 'The above quotation shows...'.
* Don't use slang or colloquialisms.
* Don't try to write everything you know about *To Kill a Mockingbird*.
* Don't misspell the names of characters or places in the novel.
* Don't confuse Harper Lee, the author of *To Kill a Mockingbird*, with Scout, her fictional narrator.
* Don't overlook the importance of writing within the time available.
* Don't forget to leave yourself a few minutes at the end to check your spelling and punctuation.

Sample essays

Question 1

To what extent is Atticus presented as a good father and citizen?

Grade C essay

1 Strong introduction

Atticus Finch's wife has died. Scout, who is telling the story, tells the reader a lot about her father, a single parent.[1] She mentions his faults too. 'Atticus was feeble: he was nearly fifty,' she says before describing the mad dog incident. Then she says that he wears glasses. 'He did not do the things our schoolmates' fathers did: he never went hunting, he did not play poker or drink or smoke. He sat in the living-room and read.'

2 Spelling mistake

3 Colloquialism
4 Shows under-standing of context

Scout is an exact contempry[2] of Harper Lee, the author. Lee's father, like Atticus, was an Alabama lawyer. Harper Lee is probably writing a bit of[3] autobiography and creating an ideal father and citizen.[4]

Jem chops down Mrs Dubose's camellias because he is distressed after the old lady says Atticus is 'lawing for niggers'. Atticus tells off Jem and sends him alone to apologise. Another time, Atticus makes Scout apologise to Aunt Alexandra for rudeness: 'as long as your aunt's in the house you do as she tells you,' he says.

5 Colloquialism
6 Good use of evidence

7 Colloquialism

Yet most of the time he is warm and there for Scout.[5] 'I ran to Atticus for comfort,' Scout says [6] after being smacked by Uncle Jack for fighting with her cousin Francis. When Jem returns from apologising to Mrs Dubose, Scout is having a cuddle with her dad. [7]

Atticus is wise as a father too, which Harper Lee shows us. He tells them what 'compromise' and 'entailment' mean. He talks to the children about his work and makes them understand why he has to defend Tom Robinson.

8 Quotation too long

He says 'when you and Jem are grown, maybe you'll look back on this with some compassion and some feeling that I didn't let you down. This case, Tom Robinson's case, is something that goes to the essence of a man's conscience — Scout, I couldn't go to church and worship God if I didn't try to help that man'.[8] This quotation shows that Atticus is a good father and a good citizen.

However, Atticus has different ideas to Aunt Alexandra. In Chapter 13, Atticus cannot explain Maycomb's 'caste system' to the children as his sister wants him to. The children know the adults are

9 Spelling mistake

dissageeing [9] about this, but Atticus will not side with them against their aunt. We can see another side of Atticus in the way he relates

10 Perceptive comments

to his sister. [10]

11 Incisive 'punchy' style

Outside the home, Atticus is a proper Christian. Judge Taylor knows that. That is why he asks Atticus to defend Tom Robinson so that he has a chance of a fair trial. [11]

We also see how much Miss Maudie Atkinson and the black community like Atticus and think he is a good citizen. Miss Maudie says 'We're so rarely called on to be Christians, but when we are, we've got men like Atticus to go for us.' When Atticus goes with Calpurnia (and Jem and Dill, who later describes it to Scout) to break the news of Tom's death to Helen Robinson, we see that the black people respect him too. Reverend Sykes gets the black people

12 Clumsy expression

in the gallery at the end of the trial to stand up in homage to Atticus. That's another example. [12]

13 Colloquialism

14 Quotation not linked to useful point

Yet not everyone thinks Atticus is a good guy. [13] Atticus says 'it's a sin to kill a mockingbird' [14] — meaning innocent people like Boo Radley and Tom Robinson — but he knows sometimes dangerous things have to be killed. That is why he shoots the dog. In the end,

15 Points set down without a strong argument linking them together

Bob Ewell dies too. [15]

Bob Ewell is a bad father and bad citizen. He is not like Atticus. Atticus makes a big mistake about him. He gets it seriously wrong about how dangerous Bob Ewell is to the Finches. This time, Aunt Alexandra is right. Atticus says Ewell 'got it all out of his system that

16 Spelling mistake

17 Good analysis

morning' (when he spat tobaco [16] juice all over Atticus in the post office). So, Atticus is not perfect. [17]

At the end, Harper Lee shows us Atticus being a devoted father. He is shocked because Jem is hurt and he thinks it is his fault. He will not leave his son's bedside although at the same time he helps Scout to understand about the real Boo Radley. He does not want

18 Points set down without a strong argument linking them together

to cover up what Boo has done either, so that shows he is a good citizen. He only agrees because Heck Tate will not take no for an answer. [18]

19 Reasonable conclusion

Atticus is meant to be a really good man, both with his children and with the people in the town, as I have tried to show. [19]

Grade A* essay

Atticus Finch, a single parent since the death of his wife four years before the main action of the novel begins, is presented entirely from Scout's point of view. She, of course, sees her father in a childlike manner, and notices his faults as well as his virtues because she is so close to him. 'Atticus was feeble: he was nearly fifty,' [1] she says before describing the mad dog incident, going on to tell the reader that he wore glasses and did nothing glamorous or exciting such as 'drive a dump-truck'.

Scout is an exact contemporary of her creator, Harper Lee, whose own father, like Atticus, was an Alabama lawyer. Harper Lee is probably using her own experience to present her ideal father and citizen. [2]

For example, Atticus is presented as firm but fair with his children. When Jem chops down Mrs Dubose's camellias because he is distressed by her condemnation of Atticus 'lawing for niggers,' [3] Atticus reprimands Jem in a voice 'like the winter wind' [3] and sends him alone to apologise. On another occasion, Atticus, his voice 'deadly', insists that Scout apologise to Aunt Alexandra for rudeness: 'as long as your aunt's in the house you do as she tells you,' he says. [3]

Yet most of the time he is warmly affectionate. 'I ran to Atticus for comfort,' Scout says after being smacked by Uncle Jack for fighting with her cousin Francis. When Jem returns from apologising to Mrs Dubose 'he found me still in Atticus's lap' and in the autumn, after the trial, when she tries to climb into her father's lap, he smiles and says 'You're getting so big now, I'll just have to hold a part of you.'

Harper Lee shows us Atticus's wisdom as a father too. He explains the meaning of words such as 'compromise' and 'entailment'. He talks to the children about his work and makes them understand why he has to defend Tom Robinson. He lets them learn from their mistakes. Scout later realises, for example, that Atticus knew at the time that she, Jem and Dill were trying to attract Boo Radley's attention with their games. When Jem asks why there are no women on juries, he says 'I was wondering when that'd occur to you'.

However, Atticus's values and views are often different from Aunt Alexandra's, and Harper Lee wants the reader to notice these

1 Short quotation

2 Extended introduction that makes mark-scoring points and refers closely to text as well as opening the essay

3 Short quotations all incorporated within sentences

contrasts. In Chapter 13, the author makes comedy out of Atticus's failure to explain Maycomb's 'caste system' to the children as his sister wants him to. The children are well aware that their father and aunt do not agree about this but, nonetheless, Atticus refuses to side with them against their aunt, who anyway becomes a softer, more sympathetic character after the trial is lost and Tom Robinson is dead. Atticus's relationship with his sister is another way in which Lee presents us with Atticus as a complex character, both father and citizen, whom we see in a range of contexts.

Outside the home, Atticus, a true Christian, is specifically asked to defend Tom Robinson by Judge Taylor. He agrees because, as he tells Scout, 'I couldn't go to church and worship God if I didn't try to help that man'. Judge Taylor respects Atticus's commitment to equality and justice so much that he knows that if Atticus defends him, Tom Robinson stands some chance of a fair trial.

4 Accurate use of vocabulary

We also see the high esteem [4] in which Atticus is held as a citizen through the conversations Lee presents the children having with Miss Maudie Atkinson and through the respect he attracts from the black community. 'We're so rarely called on to be Christians, but when we are, we've got men like Atticus to go for us,' Miss Maudie tells the children. That respect and admiration is palpable [4] too when Atticus goes with Calpurnia (and Jem and Dill, who later describes it to Scout) to break the news of Tom's death to Helen Robinson. Reverend Sykes bringing the black population to its feet in silent homage [4] to Atticus at the end of the trial is another example.

Yet that admiration of Atticus's citizenship is not universal. While Atticus is adamant that 'it's a sin to kill a mockingbird' — meaning people like Boo Radley and Tom Robinson — because they do nothing but 'sing', he also accepts that there are some elements in society which need to be removed for the safety of the majority. The rabid dog, which Atticus shoots, is one example. Bob Ewell is another.

Bob Ewell, unlike Atticus, is a bad father and bad citizen. He is Atticus's big error of judgement. Although normally a good judge of human behaviour, Atticus seriously underestimates the danger of Bob Ewell to the Finch family. On this occasion, Aunt Alexandra is right and Atticus is wrong. His view of human nature is too accommodating. After being spat at in the post office, Atticus

concludes of Ewell that he 'got it all out of his system that morning'. In this way, Harper Lee makes sure the characterisation of Atticus is fully rounded. He is a good father and citizen but he is also human and capable of mistakes. **5**

5 Events interpreted, not just recounted

At the end of the novel, Harper Lee shows us Atticus being a devoted father. Horrified by the danger that has injured Jem — for which Atticus blames himself — he is reluctant to leave his son's bedside, although at the same time he educates Scout about the real Boo Radley. We also see him still striving to be a good citizen. Only reluctantly does he agree to cover up Boo Radley's (justified) killing of Bob Ewell, and while he still believes it was Jem who wielded the knife in self-defence he will not hear of it. He is depicted as a man of total integrity and certainly as a good father and citizen, as I have tried to show. We have to remember, however, that — because of the way the novel is structured and narrated — he is also the most fully developed father and citizen in the novel, so our knowledge of him is deeper than it is of the other fathers and citizens it presents. **6**

6 Extended conclusion that makes mark-scoring points and refers closely to text as well as concluding the essay; emphasis on Harper Lee's achievement

Overall, the question is fully answered and referred to in every paragraph, and the essay is well expressed and free from spelling mistakes.

Question 2

The trial of Tom Robinson is a clear example of racial prejudice at work. Examine the different forms of prejudice that occur in the novel. How has Harper Lee made her own views about prejudice clear?

Grade C essay

Scout thinks 'there's just one kind of folks. Folks' because she is a child and is not prejudiced. *To Kill a Mockingbird* is about racism and other forms of prejudice like community prejudice against misfits such as Boo Radley and Dolphus Raymond. Women are not equal yet either, **1** so they are not allowed on juries. Aunt Alexandra thinks the Cunninghams are 'trash' because they are poor and cannot read and write. There is prejudice in favour of white people, even someone like Bob Ewell who drinks and knocks his daughter about. **2**

1 Poorly expressed

2 Loose introduction; colloquialisms

3 Spelling mistake
4 Colloquialism and poor grammar

5 Colloquialism

Tom Robinson is acused **3** of raping Mayella Ewell but he never done it. **4** He only gets a sort-of **5** fair trial because Atticus is his lawyer. Mr Gilmer, who's on the other side **5**, just goes along with the prejudices of the jury. He sneers at Tom for doing stuff [5] for Mayella. He says 'I felt right sorry for her, she seemed to try more'n the rest of 'em — ' Mr Gilmer pounces on this. In this community, a black man is not serposed [6] to feel sympathy for a white woman. When Dill cries because this upsets him, Harper Lee is showing us that Mr Gilmer is immoral although he should know better, being a lawyer like Atticus. For Tom, it's a tragedy.

6 Spelling mistake

Prejudice in the courtroom is not just against blacks. It also works in favour of Bob Ewell because he is white. Tom is a good man with a wife and children but he is black. Bob Ewell is bad. He is violent and his children are filthy (Burris with head lice at school, for example). He spends his dole money on booze [7] and probably sexually abuses Mayella ('She says what her papa do to her don't count'). But Ewell is white, so they think he is better than Tom. [8]

7 Colloquialism

8 Argument not well structured

Lee reminds us that sometimes racial prejudice works both ways. When Lula rounds on Calpurnia for bringing 'white chillun' to First Purchase Church, we feel a bit sorry for her. Harper Lee means that if you treat a group of people like rubbish, some of them will argue back. The incident helps to make *To Kill a Mockingbird* a balanced novel.

There is also prejudice against Boo Radley. He does not go out and people talk about him. For people like the gossipy Miss Stephanie Crawford, he is wicked or frightning, [9] so the children hear this and think it is true. That is why they play games about Boo and try to make him come out. But at the end we find out he is really harmless and quiet — just a bit simple. [10] Harper Lee means that you should not believe everything people say.

9 Spelling mistake

10 Colloquialism

Aunt Alexandra upsets Scout by saying the Cunninghams are 'trash'. 'But they're not our kind of folks,' she says. Is she telling Scout something sensible or is Harper Lee against class prejudice too? Aunt Alexandra's point is that 'Finch women aren't interested in that sort of people.' She does not want Scout mixing with them. Then Jem wonders why, if people are 'all alike, why do they go out of their way to despise each other?' and tries to explain to Scout.

Only men could be on juries in the Southern states in the 1930s. Scout asks Atticus why 'people like us and Miss Maudie' do not sit

11 Colloquialism

12 Spelling mistake

13 Poorly expressed

14 Not enough focus on how Lee makes her own views clear

15 Conclusion does not add anything

on juries. Even Atticus cannot resist having a dig [11] about women interupting. [12] He also thinks the idea is to 'protect' women from hearing horrible things in court. But it is not fair that cases are heard by people who know each other because they meet down the shops and other business. They cannot help having prejudice about each other. [13] Prejudice is a big theme in *To Kill a Mockingbird*. Harper Lee does not like it as she shows in her novel. [14] She makes characters say and do things to make her meaning clear. [15]

Grade A* essay

Prejudice means pre-judgement or making up your mind about something because of a preconceived view and without looking open-mindedly at the evidence. That is exactly what the jury does at the trial of Tom Robinson. Harper Lee who, like Scout, believes on the whole 'there's just one kind of folks. Folks' also makes us think, as we read *To Kill a Mockingbird,* about other forms of prejudice. These include black prejudice against white people, community prejudice against misfits such as Boo Radley and Dolphus Raymond, prejudice against women who talk too much and who are not permitted to sit on juries, class prejudice by someone like Aunt Alexandra who regards, say, the Cunninghams as 'trash' because they are poor and illiterate and, perhaps most interestingly, prejudice in favour of white people — even when

1 Strong introduction

someone is as dangerous as the lying, lazy Bob Ewell. [1]

Tom Robinson, wrongfully accused of raping Mayella Ewell, only gets a relatively fair hearing because Atticus does everything he can to bring out the truth clearly in court. His opponent, prosecuting counsel Mr Gilmer, just plays to the prejudices of the jury and most of the white onlookers in court. He ridicules Tom's neighbourly habit of doing chores for Mayella. 'I was just tryin' to help her out,' Tom says, and then: 'I felt right sorry for her, she seemed to try more'n the rest of 'em —'

Mr Gilmer pounces on this and Scout tells us, 'Below us, nobody liked Tom Robinson's answer.' The prejudices of this community are such that it is simply not acceptable for a black man to feel sympathy for a white woman. Shortly after this, Dill begins to weep, moved by the dreadful injustice of it. Scout takes him out of court and we sense that this is Harper Lee's way of stressing that Gilmer, an educated white man, has casually condemned the innocent 'mockingbird' in the dock because that is what the segregated society of 1930s Alabama expects and requires. When the jury finds Tom guilty — after longer deliberations than usual, which is some progress — we see the reactions of the children. Jem weeps and the black community is dignified and grateful. Atticus is exhausted. Harper Lee presents all the initial reaction to the verdict through the losers and so makes us aware that this is a true tragedy.

Prejudice in the courtroom is not just against Tom Robinson because he is black. It also works in favour of Bob Ewell because he is white. Harper Lee makes her feelings clear here because the characters she has created are extreme examples of good and bad. Tom is a respectable, hard-working family man with a wife and three children but he is black. Bob Ewell is the violent father of seven filthy, neglected children (Burris with head lice who disrupts school, for example), who spends his welfare cheque on drink and probably sexually abuses Mayella ('She says what her papa do to her don't count,' Tom tells the court about Mayella's attempt to seduce him) — but Ewell is white. [2] As Scout sums it up for Harper Lee, 'in the secret courts of men's hearts Atticus had no case. Tom was a dead man the minute Mayella Ewell opened her mouth and screamed.'

2 Uses evidence well

Only once in the novel does Lee remind us that sometimes racial prejudice works both ways. When Lula rounds on Calpurnia for bringing 'white chillun' to First Purchase Church, we feel a shred of sympathy for her although she is overridden by Calpurnia and Reverend Sykes. Harper Lee is showing us that if you treat a group of people as underlings, even though in law they are supposed to have equality, some of them will try to turn the tables and that is understandable. The incident helps to make *To Kill a Mockingbird* a balanced novel. [3]

3 Sustained argument reviews several sorts of prejudice

Another major form of prejudice in the novel works against Boo Radley because he is a recluse and there are rumours about him. [4] For people like the gossip-loving Miss Stephanie Crawford, he must therefore be wicked or frightening. The children, not yet old enough to know better, take this idea and play with it at the beginning of the novel. By revealing the real Boo Radley as harmless, gentle, shy and damaged to Scout and to the reader at the end of the novel, Harper Lee shows us that most prejudices are based on falsehood.

4 Sustained argument reviews several sorts of prejudice

5 Sustained argument reviews several sorts of prejudice

She does the same thing in a more minor way with Dolphus Raymond. [5] Everyone thinks he's 'in the clutches of whiskey'. In fact, outside the courthouse during the trial, Scout and Dill discover for themselves that the drink he carries around with him is nothing stronger than Coca-Cola. Lee's message is surely to examine the evidence before you make a judgement.

Aunt Alexandra upsets Scout by condemning the Cunninghams as 'trash' and refusing to allow Scout to invite Walter to the house. 'But they're not our kind of folks,' she says, explaining that 'you can scrub Walter Cunningham till he shines, you can put him in shoes and a new suit, but he'll never be like Jem'. Is she telling Scout something that is actually reasonable or is Harper Lee condemning class prejudice too

6 Sustained argument reviews several sorts of prejudice

? [6] After all, Atticus sat at the table with Walter a year or two earlier when Jem invited him to lunch on Scout's first day at school. He talked to him courteously and Calpurnia insisted that Scout did too. Aunt Alexandra's point is that 'Finch women aren't interested in that sort of people,' so she does not want Scout mixing with them. Then Harper Lee has Jem, who wonders why if people are 'all alike, they go out of their way to despise each other?' trying to explain it to Scout.

Juries in the Southern states of the 1930s were all male, to Scout's indignation. In a conversation with Atticus, intended to draw the reader's attention to this prejudice which was over by the time the novel was published in 1960, Scout asks why 'people like us and Miss Maudie' do not sit on juries. Even Atticus cannot resist a quip about women interrupting. More seriously, he guesses (without condemnation) that the idea is to 'protect' women from sordid cases. Through his explanation to the children about small-town life — everyone knowing everyone, shopping, money and local interests — we realise that a case is being made against the injustice of people being tried by juries who are known to them and therefore prejudiced in some way.

Prejudice and attitudes to it is a major theme in *To Kill a Mockingbird*, which Harper Lee explores from a range of angles. Maycomb is an insular society, 'a tired old town' steeped in racial prejudice and its 'caste system'. Apart from the possible exception of needing to be realistic about class differences, the author seems to be arguing strongly against it and makes her feelings clear through Scout's observations and her reports of what other characters say and do.

The essay is well expressed, with accurate punctuation and spelling.

How to get an A* grade

To get an A* grade, you must:

* answer the question fully or do exactly what the task asks you to do
* construct a clear argument or line of reasoning
* make good use of frequent short quotations within your sentences
* shape your answer by planning it with an introduction and a conclusion
* express your ideas in good English
* write clearly, with precision and in an appropriate tone
* spell accurately

Review your learning

1 What is meant by 'textual evidence'?
2 What is the main difference between a higher-tier question and a foundation-tier question?
3 What are the three main things that GCSE questions on *To Kill a Mockingbird* are likely to focus on?
4 How will you set about devising an essay plan?
5 What might you include in:
  a an essay introduction?
  b an essay conclusion?
6 What are the main differences between a grade C answer and an A* answer?

Answers

Answers to 'Review your learning' questions.

Context (page 13)

1 She was born in Monroeville, Alabama in 1926, the youngest of three children. Their father was a lawyer.
2 The Northerners banned slavery. The Southern states, including Alabama, wanted it to continue, so they tried to break away from the North to form the Confederate States. The Northerners would not allow this.
3 Martin Luther King Jr
4 It created high unemployment and poverty — the Depression.
5 The arrest, in 1931, of nine young black men in Scottsboro, Alabama, who were found guilty of rape. The charges were later disproved.
6 'Southern values' generally mean that, however bad things are, you must defend your honour. They also involve a pride in family ancestry, especially in families with an aristocratic background. Most negatively, in the 1930s they included racist attitudes.
7 Southern novels tend to be regional and to present a strong sense of place. They also convey a feeling of loneliness and isolation. They show a pride in tradition but criticise racial prejudice. Southern novels also often present guilt.
8 The answer is up to you, but it could include Lee's desire to expose the evil of prejudice in all its forms and to try to explain its origins.
9 The answer requires an opinion, but some of the novel's appeal almost certainly lies in the following: its strong characterisation and the appeal of its characters; its dry humour; good storytelling, with strong elements of suspense and mystery; its appeal to the better side of human nature.

Plot and structure (page 35)

1 Miss Maudie
2 a Jimmy
   b Francis
3 Mr Link Deas
4 The 'defendant' is Dill. Atticus has to persuade his family to let him stay with the Finch family after he runs away from home.

5 Reverend Sykes makes the black people in the gallery stand up to show respect for Atticus as he leaves the court at the end of the trial.

6 This is a matter of personal interpretation. However, be aware that the novel is in two parts. In Part Two, Jem is bordering on adolescence and is beginning to grow apart from Scout. Significant events include:

* the children's attempts to make Boo Radley come out, and the presents he leaves them in the hollow tree, which stop when his brother Nathan fills in the hole
* Miss Maudie's house burning down
* Atticus shooting the rabid dog, which influences the children's view of him (especially Jem's)
* Jem having to read to Mrs Dubose
* Aunt Alexandra coming to stay
* the trial and death of Tom Robinson
* Bob Ewell's attack on the children
* Scout finally meeting Boo Radley

7 This question has no single correct answer. However, you could argue for either the trial's 'guilty' verdict or the attack on the children by Bob Ewell as being the climax.

Characterisation (page 56)

1 Miss Maudie (of Atticus)
2 Boo Radley
3 Cecil Jacobs, Francis, Mrs Dubose
4 She is critical of Scout's tomboyishness and Atticus's upbringing of her.
5 Reverend Sykes and Calpurnia speak to the children about Tom and his family at First Purchase Church. Atticus talks to them about Tom, and Jem is with Atticus when he goes to tell Helen that Tom has been killed.
6 He has no good features in his character.
7 Miss Stephanie Crawford
8 She shows the characters speaking, acting and responding. She allows us to share Scout's responses at first hand. If Scout is surprised, puzzled or delighted, so are we. Lee also uses humour.
9 This is a matter of opinion, but remember that Scout is the narrator as well as being a major character. On the other hand, there is a great deal of close focus on Atticus and Jem.

Themes (page 68)

1 An idea, or set of ideas, threaded through a piece of writing.
2 Racism, family, mockingbirds, courage and growing up.

3 Tom Robinson and Boo Radley

4 Moral courage

5 The suffering caused by racist ignorance.

6 This could be any of the children, but Jem is a strong contender.

Style (page 76)

1 First-person narrative

2 The first-person narrator can describe at first hand only things that he or she has personally witnessed. Scout cannot be present at every event in the novel. Lee gets around this by having other characters report events to Scout.

3 The racism that fuels the novel's two central events (the rape trial and Ewell's attack on the children) was a feature of the Southern states. A feature of the small-town setting is that everyone knows everyone else and can comment on them.

4 * To establish character. Calpurnia's 'hand was as wide as a bed slat and twice as hard'. Mayella's nervousness is stressed by Scout's description of her as 'a steady-eyed cat with a twitchy tail' (Chapter 18).

  * To convey feeling, as in Scout's distaste for Mrs Dubose: 'Her face was the colour of a dirty pillowcase, and the corners of her mouth glistened with wet, which inched like a glacier down the deep grooves enclosing her chin' (Chapter 11).

  * To evoke a sense of place. An example is the Ewell's home being like 'the playhouse of an insane child' (Chapter 17).

  * Linked to symbolism, as in the mockingbird of the title, a metaphor for innocence and vulnerability.

5 Uncle Jack is an educated man living in the North. Mr Cunningham is a poor, uneducated farmer from the South. 'Her use of invective leaves nothing to the imagination' (Uncle Jack, Chapter 9). 'It was obstreperous, disorderly and abusive' (Uncle Jack, Chapter 9). 'Mr Finch, I don't know when I'll ever be able to pay you' (Mr Cunningham, Chapter 2). 'I'll tell him you said hey, little lady' (Mr Cunningham, Chapter 15).

6 Suspense is built up by the words 'whispered' and 'sneaked'. The words 'sneaked' and 'peeked' also suggest the actions and language of children. The description makes the reader identify with the experience of the children, who observe the men but do not know why they are there. We get a sense of uncertainty, suspense and menace from the image of shadows becoming substance. The simple 'He in there, Mr Finch?' reveals that the man is probably an uneducated farmer (he does not ask 'Is he in there?') and that he knows Atticus will know why the men are there.

Tackling the exam (page 93)

1 Textual evidence is the use of quotations, or references, to events or descriptions from the novel to back up your answers.

2 Foundation-tier questions have bullet points to help you construct an answer; higher-tier questions do not.

3 Plot, character and theme

4 Work out what you think the question is asking to you to do. Highlight key words in the question. Jot down your main ideas and number them in order.

5 a How you are going to tackle the question, your interpretation of the question or a comment on something in it.

   b A summary of your arguments, or a paragraph drawing them together in a new way — a new point you have held back for the ending.

6 See 'How to get an A* grade' on page 93.